LIVING
LIFE

VIA

THE SILVER CORD

VALERIE HUTCHINGS

ISBN 978-1-0980-4604-0 (paperback)
ISBN 978-1-0980-4605-7 (digital)

Christian Faith Publishing, Inc.
832 Park Avenue
Meadville, PA 16335
www.christianfaithpublishing.com

Printed in the United States of America

This book is about how God *really* talks to us.

If you've ever "gone with your gut" to make a decision or felt "butterflies in your stomach" when nervous, you're likely getting signals from an unexpected source: your *second* brain. Hidden in the walls of the digestive system, this "brain in your gut" is revolutionizing medicine's understanding of the links between digestion, mood, health, and even the way you think (https://www.Hopkinsmedicine.org/health/wellness-and-prevention/the-brain-gut-connection).

We are connected in an unseen way. I know because I've seen it. And God would not reveal this to me until 2009… But first…

I am by all means a "nobody." But God is no respecter of persons. What I have to share is what God has placed in my "gut" my whole life. If anyone has ever "felt led," a Southern term for doing the Lord's work, it just could be the voice of God telling you to do something, or it could be your gut, in ways you've not heard or you're not even aware of. This book is my testimony of how I have listened to God and lived the plan that God has for me. Since I'm still here, alive and kicking, God's plan for me is far from over. To have this book published would be a little girl's "dream" come true—to be a part of the solution and not the problem. I've lived a gut-led ambition my whole life. However, sometimes one has to live a lifetime before one can share.

I truly believe that not only did God know Jeremiah before he was born—"Before I formed you in the womb I knew you, before you were born I set you apart; I appointed you as a prophet to the nations" (Jer. 1:5)—but God also *knew* all of us. And he has a plan for all of us as well while we are on earth. In heaven, while our spirits are still with God, everything is perfect. We think, *I can do this! But* when we arrive and realize we are clothed in a human body and we are naked and helpless, all of a sudden we realize we only have our five senses that are still to be developed! The stark reality hits us, and we perceive we are not humans having a spiritual experience, but spirits having a very human experience! We will need a lot more than that to survive. No wonder we cry. And because our memories are "erased" by the physical world, we must learn to hear God's voice again. Most of us never learn this. I hope this book will inspire others to learn how to do just that: "Because narrow is the gate, and narrow is the way, which leads unto life, and few there be that find it" (Matt. 7:14 AKJV).

The following is a *fact*:

> But Jesus answered, "It is written: 'Man shall not live on bread alone, but on every word that comes from the mouth of God.'" (Matt. 4:4)

We have refused to listen to our book of instructions: the Bible. Some modern Christians believe the Old Testament (OT) was simply the word of man and is fallible. However, the apostle Paul viewed the OT as the infallible word of God. Below, we will use scriptural quotations followed by comments to show why this is true:

"All Scripture is God-breathed and is useful for teaching, rebuking, correcting and training in righteousness, so that the servant of God may be thoroughly equipped for every good work" (2 Tim. 3:16–17). This is a confirmation that the Bible *is* for life's instructions.

The apostle Paul affirms God's active involvement in the writing of the Scripture, an involvement so powerful and pervasive that what is written is the infallible and authoritative word of God (bibleauthenticity.com).

This book is the testimony/journey of my life as I've tried to listen to the plan/mission (the work assigned to me) through my "gut," as one might say, or "intuition": how I have learned what my spiritual gifts are, how I've used them to the best of my ability, and how, as an example, others should learn to know and use them, especially today. The harder the battle or overcoming the problems we are faced with, the higher the calling. I've seen this in testimony after testimony. Not all of us have had to take drugs and overcome them to find that calling. Some of us just have to find ourselves through the mess of life.

How many of us have truly listened to God? The condition of the world should tell us. Hopefully, this book will help people be more aware, that it's not too late, that they too can learn to listen to that still small voice that speaks to all of us. Max Lucado's book *In the Grip of Grace* is a fantastic explanation of how the world looks at religion. That is why one of this book's "missions" is to illuminate that "God should not be viewed as a religion." He is God, and no one should or can put him into a religious box and limit his power or the power that is in each of us.

* * * * *

This world is far from Eden. In fact, there are many believers who believe we are closer to the end days than ever before.

> This know also, that in the last days perilous times shall come.
>
> For men shall be lovers of their own selves, covetous, boasters, proud, blasphemers, disobedient to parents, unthankful, unholy,
>
> Without natural affection, trucebreakers, false accusers, incontinent, fierce, despisers of those that are good,
>
> Traitors, heady, highminded, lovers of pleasures more than lovers of God;
>
> Having a form of godliness, but denying the power thereof: from such turn away. (2 Tim. 3:1–5 KJV)

I know, I know.! People have been saying this for hundreds of years. It took Noah over a hundred years to build the ark. He was mocked and scorned the whole time because there had never been any rain!

Genesis 2:5-6 states, "When the Lord God made the universe, there were no plants on the earth and no seeds had sprouted, because he had not sent any rain."

I guess they changed their minds real quick when it did start to rain.

From the dispensation of Moses leading God's chosen people from the bondage of Egypt until the great flood was two thousand years. From Noah until Jesus was another two thousand years. From Jesus's death and resurrection, it's been two thousand years. That is a total of six thousand years, give or take a few years.

> Thus the heavens and the earth were finished, and all the host of them.
> And on the seventh day God finished his work that he had done, and he rested on the seventh day from all his work that he had done.
> So God blessed the seventh day and made it holy, because on it God rested from all his work that he had done in creation. (Gen. 2:2)

In Genesis 1:5, 8, 13, 19, 23, and 31, each day is described as having an evening and a morning. These two words, *evening* and *morning*, literally mean dusk and dawn. This clearly shows that in this instance, each day is a literal twenty-four-hour period. Continuing with the thought of literal days, we go on to read in Genesis 2:1–3, God blessed and sanctified a literal day, the Sabbath, as the day he ceased from his labors (answers from The Book Net (on Facebook)

There is a seventh day coming for this earth, and it will be a day of a thousand years. God's creation was to echo redemption by defining a day as one thousand years (Ps. 90:4; 2 Pet. 3:8 quoted above). From beginning to end, it was determined by God that mankind was to have only six days (six thousand years) to live out his time on earth. On the seventh day, the day of the Lord (millennium), God himself would intervene into human affairs and usher in the kingdom of God on earth (Christianforums.com).

The Bible is an "instruction manual" for how each and every one of us should live. We wouldn't put together any bike or do-it-yourself project without reading the instructions, yet people do not want to be "preached to." The Word of God is a proven fact, by its very own words, the OT foretelling of the New Testament. It's not preaching. The Bible is here to teach.

God's promises to us are *not* of war and hatred or fear and lack: "For I know the plans I have for you, declares the LORD, plans to prosper you and not to harm you, to give you a future and a hope" (Jer. 29:11).

* * * * *

I was eight years old when God started "talking" to me (1958). Eight is the biblical number, according to Don Kistler in his book *The Arithmetic of God*, for "new beginnings." This book, presenting the mathematical structure of the Bible, was given by inspiration of the Holy Ghost. The Author is the alpha and the omega. His name is Yeshua, Salvation, Jesus Christ by which all things were created. He is the Father, Son, and Holy Ghost. The Author brings forth the Word of God so that the truth comes to revelation and leads one to know that the Spirit cannot be seen, but Jesus Christ is the Spirit. The living Word of God becomes alive and reveals himself as spirit and truth and shall come again in glory. Words can be changed and given private interpretation, but numbers remain the same in all languages and dialects.

I remember where I was. I was in third grade and was in the classroom, and everything around me went into slow motion. This is when I had a very distinct memory and sense of urgency that time was running out. I knew I had to do something! But I was only eight years old. God had also given me a very important message. I had an out-of-body experience when I was just a couple of years younger (1956–1957) and would not find out what it meant until the year 2009.

Not only did God make me aware that there were things that needed to be done, but he also told me that my husband's name was

Jim—something I didn't need to know right then. I had no idea what I would be able to do or could even do, where to start with my "assignment," or whatever it was God needed for me to do. I didn't even have a car! I was only eight years old!

There were three Jims in our class. To keep them apart, the teacher assigned each of them their own version of "Jim": one was Jim, another Jimmy, and another James. Therefore, the one whom I knew as Jim, as an eight-year-old, was not my choice for a husband; and I told God, "I don't want to marry Jim. He picks his nose and eats it!"

God had a laugh like thunder. I was really upset, but he told me that I had a long time before I was to marry, to which I wondered, "Why did you tell me now then?" There were many things God would teach me along my life's journey and in God's timing, and not when I think I needed to know. God telling me that my husband's name "was Jim" was my first experience with prophecy from God.

* * * * *

I have always had a heart for the underdog. In school, I *was* the underdog, but that did not stop me from doing what I could to make a difference for any problem that I was aware of. I wanted to be a part of the solution and not the problem because of what God told me. I also desired to be accepted because I was not, even at home. This was *Knowing* One's Purpose 101, lessons of life's beginning, without fully understanding. Innocence and lack of knowledge will and can destroy one unless the line of communication is kept open between the pupil and the teacher, and/*or* the teacher has a plan for the pupil. Every single one of us is connected to the teacher: God. But God has shown me *how* we are truly connected. And it's so real and yet so unseen.

Despite being bullied and called every name in the book, and coming home, getting off the bus, and crying all the way up the hill to our house and wishing I were dead, I persisted in trying to do what God would have me do. *This* was bigger than me.

Again, I say I believe that not only did God know Jeremiah before he was formed in his mother's womb (Jer. 1:5), but God also knew all of us, and we picked our destiny while on earth. In heaven, everything is perfect, and spirits can only relate to heaven. However, when having to live in flesh, our spiritual eyes are blinded, and we see through a glass darkly: "But then face to face; now I know in part; but then shall I know even as also I am known" (1 Cor. 13:12). And when we arrive in this world, not only are we naked, we're helpless! We're going to have to rely on complete strangers for everything! Some of us are loved and adored and nurtured, and others are not so lucky. We are all overcomers, no matter what color we are or what status life gives us: "To him who overcomes I will give some of the hidden manna to eat. And I will give him a white stone, and on the stone a new name written, which no one knows except him who receives it" (Rev. 2:17).

While here on earth, in flesh, it's very easy to give over to the five senses and forget our mission, God's ultimate plan for us. As an eight-year-old, I was completely clueless. However, that never stopped an overwhelming desire to do what I had to do. There was something inside of me that was bigger than me and urging me to do good, to be a part of the solution and not the problem.

* * * * *

On August 5, 1950, at precisely 3:35 a.m., the breath of God came into the Little Traverse Hospital in Petoskey, Michigan, where I took my first breath. The umbilical cord was cut, and another (unseen and more important one) began…

I believe that children are a fresh breath from God with empty pages to be written on all the days of their lives and that one should be very careful what words are put toward those pages. And unless we stay childlike—big difference from being childish—we shall not enter into the kingdom of God: "And said, Truly I say to you, unless you are converted and become like children, you will not enter the kingdom of heaven" (Matt. 18:3). Being childlike is trusting your father who is in heaven to know what's best for you and not letting

9

your pride/thoughts and understanding get in the way. Just as a child trusts their parents for everything vital in their life, we need to trust our creator for all things: "For it was you who formed my inward parts; you knit me together in my mother's womb" (Ps. 139:13).

Science has not proven this; but in my humble opinion, just as our fingerprints make us unique, we are marked in other ways. I'm not condoning or even believing in the reading of palms. However, I have noticed (and it's been proven in instances of reincarnation) that people bear the marks of their death in scars. So how hard would it be to believe that God marks us in other ways? It took a long time for me to realize that I have "birthmarks," not a mole or scar, but the blood that runs through my hands, in my veins. On my left hand, it spells, in Hebrew, Yahweh and on my right hand, a two-inch-long and one-and-a-half-inch-wide heart! God made me this way.

God gave me the scripture when I was very young: "For our struggle is not against flesh and blood, but against the rulers, against the authorities, against the powers of this dark world and against the spiritual forces of evil in the heavenly realms. Therefore put on the full armor of God, so that when the day of evil comes, you may be able to stand your ground" (Eph. 6:12–13).

And by my mother's way of teaching me of what not to be, by her hypocritical actions, I learned to watch my words. I am an over-comer, not of drugs and sex, but of thoughts of suicide and people, because of their lack of knowledge, their lies, and their betrayals. I have had people spit on me and throw me from homes (for speaking truth) and even plot to kill me. My story proceeds…

Masaru Emoto's books prove how strong and how powerful our words are. In his book *The Hidden Messages in Water*, Masaru shows with pictures the effects of how, when one just speaks to water, it affects that drop of water. If we as humans are made up of 67 percent water, wouldn't words have the same affect? Psalm 139:14 reads, "I will praise thee: for I am fearfully and wonderfully made: marvelous are thy works; and that my soul knoweth right well."

Most importantly, God's word tells us that the tongue is a cre-ative force: "The power of the tongue is life and death—those who love to talk will eat what it produces" (Prov. 18:21). Death and life are in the power of the tongue, and those who love its use will eat its fruit. *The Tongue: A Creative Force* by Charles Capps is an excellent book on the power of the tongue.

Words are powerful and should be used by allowing the taming of the Holy Spirit: "A gentle tongue is a tree of life, but perverseness in it breaks the spirit" (Prov. 15:4). In this final Bible verse about taming the tongue, Solomon sees a gentle tongue as one that gives life; but when used in a perverse or evil manner, it breaks the person's spirit. People need to know that the Holy Spirit is capable of teaching us godly ways, if only we choose to ask.

How many have had their spirits broken by unkind words? They turn to alcohol and drugs to ease the pain. This book is not about how I was rescued from drugs, but how I kept the faith in my ignorance and childlike obedience/faith.

Again, I say, God says in Revelations 3:21, "To him that overcometh will I grant to sit with me in my throne, even as I also overcame, and am set down with my Father in his throne."

I have been overcoming all my life and know that we are all here, not for us, but for the will of God. We all have a plan that is of God, and we must all learn how to overcome the enemy of God. I emphasize the following:

> Put on the whole armour of God, that ye may be able to stand against the wiles of the devil.
>
> For we wrestle not against flesh and blood, but against principalities, against powers, against the rulers of the darkness of this world, against spiritual wickedness in high places.
>
> Wherefore take unto you the whole armour of God, that ye may be able to withstand in the evil day, and having done all, to stand.
>
> Stand therefore, having your loins girt about with truth, and having on the breastplate of righteousness;

And your feet shod with the preparation of the gospel of peace;

Above all, taking the shield of faith, wherewith ye shall be able to quench all the fiery darts of the wicked.

And take the helmet of salvation, and the sword of the Spirit, which is the word of God:

Praying always with all prayer and supplication in the Spirit, and watching thereunto with all perseverance and supplication for all saints. (Eph. 6:11–18 KJV)

Our enemy is in the spiritual world that exists in a dimension unseen by the natural eye. (This is what I will explain later that happened to me personally.)

Our communication is unseen, but not to God, and not to our enemy, Satan. This is Satan's "world." He was cast here until Jesus comes back. Although Satan cannot be omnipresent, he has the legions of demons under precise control, and they are very well organized. *Placebo*, by Howard Pittman, will tell you exactly how real the spirit world is and how heinous and organized Satan's demons are, how they are allowed possess a human, and how they do Satan's will through that person.

In Betty Malz's book *My Glimpse of Eternity*, she speaks of our prayers. While in heaven, she was amazed by something that resembled the northern lights or airport beacons. "These were prayers ascending from the earth," she noted. "They were ascending like laser beams, going directly to the light in the throne room."

Radio waves are unseen, but they are never ending and are able to pass through solid objects and billions of light-years. Scientists have proven this.

Jesus was sent and came to do his Father's will. He was God all wrapped up in an itty-bitty human with phenomenal powers and gave those powers to us.

When asked by the Pharisees when the kingdom of God would come, Jesus replied, "The kingdom of God will not come with observable signs. Nor will people say, 'Look, here it is,' or 'There it is.' For you see, the kingdom of God is in your midst." Then He said to the disciples, "The time is coming when you will long to see one of the days of the Son of Man, but you will not see it… For indeed, the kingdom of God is within you." (Luke 17:20–21)

One must learn to know and say the Lord's Prayer *correctly*: "After this manner therefore pray ye: Our Father which art in heaven, Hallowed be thy name. Thy kingdom come. **Thy will be done IN earth**, as [it is] in heaven. Give us this day our daily bread. And forgive us our debts, as we forgive our debtors. And lead us not into temptation, but deliver us from evil: For thine is the kingdom, and the power, and the glory, for ever. Amen" (Matt. 6:9–13; emphasis mine). We are the earthen vessels through which God will work, *if* we choose to let him, while we are *on* this earth.

The Bible is so true on its words: "Man shall not live by bread alone, but by every word that proceedeth out of the mouth of God" (Matt. 4:4). And oh, how we do! My aunt, who never went to church, once told me that she believed that "idle words often come to pass." She'd seen it happen.

The condition of this world we live in now is proof that words matter. We get what we speak! I have often heard people say, "I think I'm catching a cold." Why would anyone want to "catch a cold"? Yet they do! This is just a sample of how powerful our words can be!

Everything that God created, he spoke first, and then it was. Just read the very first book of the Bible, Genesis! Everything in heaven is more real and eternal than what we are seeing and living now. All we see can be destroyed. Heaven is eternal.

I have never been materialistic. Right now, because I am "aware," I believe that everything I see, I "own." Thank God I don't have to take it home and keep it, dust it, clean it, pay for it, or worry about someone stealing it. My basic needs have always been met—sometimes too much. I don't take up much space, was born without anything, and will die the same way. What I learn in between is what we are all here for. I have always praised God for everything I am blessed with. Even when I don't feel like thanking God for something, I praise God anyway. If I don't, then the enemy, Satan, has got me right where he wants me. Resisting him makes him flee; Satan cannot stand faith. He wants you to live in fear and doubt and unbelief, and all the while he steals your peace and prosperity. In God's words, "The thief [Satan] comes only to steal and kill and destroy; I have come so that they may have life, and may have it abundantly" (John 10:10 New Heart English Bible).

We speak and then we create, in more ways than one. We form an idea and it becomes reality. One speaks his day's existence every day. What have you spoken today?

Clam Lake

Clam Lake is one of the Chain O'Lakes that lie nestled between the tips of the little and ring finger of Michigan, winding and sparkling like a strand of dew-dropped spider's web.

Grass River, a shallow, snakelike, and grassy river, paralleled on either side by gently rustling, whispering pines, is the source from which Clam Lake originates. Clam Lake, shaped like a bucking kidney bean, with a straight tail, is approximately three miles long and one quarter mile wide. I considered it my favorite aunt and uncle's backyard.

It is also surrounded by swaying whispering pines that seem to hold up the sky, all hiding cozy, little-windowed cottages at their feet. White sandy paths run down from the cottages to the edge of the lake and out onto tonguelike docks that stick out into the water.

On a lazy summer's day, it is a common sight and sound to see and hear what starts out to be a deep-voiced fly, turning out to be a lazily driven motorboat, sputtering along and pulling a fan of rippling water as it fills the air with the pungent odors of oil and gas.

As I look across the lake, it is only an illusion that the water appears sky blue as it wrinkles and glistens with the dancing of sun diamonds. Actually, its depths hold many colored and awesome secrets.

Climbing into a rowboat, I can hear the steady, gentle lapping of the waves as they wash the shore.

Near the shore, as I look into the depths, I can see that the water is as clear as it can be but is mucky and turned brown when touched. It is covered with sunken and abandoned clam shells, snake grass, long flat fingers of slimy seaweed swaying gently with the undercurrents, and tall green slender poles reaching up and balancing lily pad plates that hold white-petaled teacup flowers.

Occasionally, I will see a turtle's head sticking up among the lily pads, trying to camouflage itself against the not-yet-opened lily buds. I may even see a snake gliding under the water or a striped perch suspended between the surface and bottom of the lake, so still except for the whisper movement of a lacy gill.

The farther I row out into the water, the greener and more eerie and captivating the waters become.

Near the beginning of the approximately five-hundred-foot-long Clam Lake, which leads into Torch Lake, on either side of the ever-narrowing lake, are long half-moon-shaped old tin buildings. They hold boats, some old, some new and a haunting display of reflecting, patchy lights dancing on water and ceiling combined with gentle bumping of boats against their berths as the water ripples in from a passing motorboat.

All this seems to be echoing a ghostly tale of a different world, long ago of sun-filled, easygoing days with laughter that floated lightly across the waters and played an enchanting melody of peace in my ears.

It was at Clam Lake I spent a lot of time daydreaming and felt close to God.

I also loved to walk in the wooded areas close to our home. There were many beautiful flowers—jack-in-the-pulpits, trilliums, violet, Dutchman's-breeches, forget-me-nots, daisies, black-eyed Susans, Queen Anne's lace, bachelor's buttons, buttercups, and wild lilacs, just to mention a few. There is nothing like a forest to be in when one visits with God. The smells and sounds will quiet one's soul. Nature is allowed to speak, and God is in nature.

* * * * *

I remember spending hours at my aunt's house. She was more like a mother to me than my own mother. This aunt was my mother's sister (ten years older than my mother); and she had never been able to have children because when my uncle was a child, he had the measles, which caused him to become sterile. Their hearts went out to me because of my mother's abuse.

They had a very old record player and lots of 78s. For those who do not know what a 78 is, it's an old vinyl record. Later on there would be 45s, and they would be much smaller with big holes in their center. And then there were cassette tapes, and then CDs and DVDs, and then iPods—the evolution of technology. I loved and played this one 78 over and over: "The Tennessee Waltz." Looking back, I truly believe it was prophetic, because it happened… The song tells a story of a woman introducing her friend to her darling, and while they were dancing, she stole him away. She wasn't my friend in the beginning or the end, but a woman did steal my husband's heart for five years, while he was still married to me (in Tennessee), and she wouldn't be the only one.

I have always said that if God is the same yesterday, today, and always, then he still uses people just as he did in biblical times. No one, back then, knew that they would be used in a book called the Bible and have it be the best-selling book of all time. "Hey! Quiet on the set… We must apply more makeup on the pharaoh… Someone please do something with Moses's hair!" It didn't happen… Just for a moment, put yourself in Joseph's shoes and ask yourself, what was he thinking all the time he was in prison for something he did not do? Imagine being Moses, who had a problem stuttering, and take time to really think what he must have wondered and thought when he found out God chose him to lead his people out of Egypt. Every single person God used, in the Bible, he had a master plan for them, just as he does for every single one of us.

No one is sure of what the population, of the "world," was in the biblical days of Joseph and the Romans. The exact population is a bit unclear. Estimates for the period fall in between two and four million. This area of Egypt was one of the more densely populated areas in the world at that time due to the fertility of the Nile delta.

In the biblical account, Exodus 12:30 says, "For there was not a house without someone dead." Family size is also tough to nail down. Based on typical ancient family structures, we can assume that the average extended family was between ten and twenty people rather than the lower numbers we see today. Thus, we can figure that the death toll was probably at least between one hundred thousand and two hundred thousand, assuming at least one death per extended family (household) with an affected population of about three million, give or take (History.stackexchange.com).

But...there were other people there besides the ones whose stories are told in the Bible. One can imagine neighbors saying, "Hey, did ya hear what happened to that big group of Egyptians living down the Nile? Wasn't there some guy named Moses who came along and really stirred things up around there?" *No!* We do not hear about things like that, and they probably didn't speak at all in that manner, but if one had a newspaper to run, and a camera to be an official news person... Those people who are in the Bible were just as human as any of us! They all bled when cut, cried when hurt, loved to be loved, and had dreams. I hope one might understand they were all as human as we are today and limited in their knowledge of how God truly works. Isaiah 55:8 states, "For my thoughts are not your thoughts, neither are your ways my ways, declares the LORD" (Isaiah55:8-9).

* * * * *

God truly has been my strength all through this life. I know my strengths, which I will share later on; but right now, as I write this book, I struggle with one of my greatest weaknesses: procrastination and the feeling of not being worthy of this assignment. However, every single day God talks to me and tells me things that are specific to the plan, the assignment of this book, so I obey even though it's a real struggle. But I know from what I am struggling against.

I mentioned earlier that I was not accepted at home. To all who knew my mother, aunts, and uncles, they knew that my mother never once defended me. There were a couple of my relatives, when I was an adult, and out of earshot of my mother, who told me that they were so sorry for my upbringing. I'm not saying that I have had it worse than others. I know there are people who have had and still are walking much harder walks than I have had to. I just want people to know that *we all have a plan that God has written specifically for us, and we have to overcome the pitfalls and struggles as individuals.* But we are not alone. We have God, Jesus, and the Holy Spirit to guide us if we choose.

There are no good memories of my childhood, yet I am blessed in comparison to the abuses of countless others. I am still blessed to this day, even though my situation is not what or where I want to be at the moment. God uses the most inopportune times in our lives to teach us our biggest lessons. Later I will continue to prove this. I need to tell about myself so that you understand what I had to overcome and deal with. There are a lot of us who feel the same way and have been treated the same way. It's not a sob story but a testimony of overcoming.

My first memory of abuse, and yes, I was emotionally abused, was when I was at the tender age of three. We had spent all day at the beach, and I had collected a half can, about the size of a liter, of butterfly shells. I was going to take them home and make many pretty things with them. But my mother would not allow it. She didn't want sand in the car. So I did what I had to do: I buried them, can and all, in the sand. After all that work, no one was going to have them. I couldn't. There was no one encouraging my abilities. A seed had been planted for failure. I will overcome.

Later, I wanted to go inside the house to use the bathroom. I had to poop (hey, I was three years old here), but my mother would not let me inside to do so. I *had* to go, so I found privacy in our neighbor's garage. It was then I found out my sister was a liar and manipulator and always would be. She spotted me and went and told my mother. I got in trouble for using the bathroom in our neighbor's garage. All the time I was at home, if I tried to tell on my sister for things that were wrong, my mother would say, "You must have done something to deserve it." I have had to choose to forgive my sister, even though she has never been sorry for her part in my rearing. It is and was part of God's plan. All my life I have been plagued by liars and manipulators. I have been fired from jobs without the ability to even know why or defend myself. I was spit on and physically thrown out of a house for being honest. I have been used and abused a lot in my life because of my gift of mercy and lack of wisdom. My second husband, the man I am with now and the father of my children, tried to kill me once and threatened to kill me after that. I even had someone else plot to kill me. Gee, imagine me being paranoid. But I trust my god to watch out for me. I *know* God has a plan for me and that he is with me.

I know that it may be hard to understand and accept that God would use negative things in his plan for us, but have you read the Bible? Did Joseph deserve to be sold into slavery by his brothers? God had a plan.

One can grow up thinking, *Why even try?* and *Maybe I did do something wrong*, even when they are innocent! It can take years to overcome these unencouraging words. I was in my forties before I found self-confidence. I am blessed that I knew better than to turn to drugs or alcohol. The problem would still be there when sober. I am blessed that "something" gave me common sense. I even wanted to change my name one time, and God told me it wouldn't make any difference. I would still be blamed. So I decided to keep my name.

I wrote a letter to Dear Abby once. She replied. I still have the letter. In it I told her how my mother treated me, and Dear Abby replied, "I'm not an expert in this area, but I think your mother may have a personality disorder… When I was 15, my mother found me with a knife in my hand, contemplating suicide. We, my mother, dad, and I, all ended up going to see a psychologist and a psychiatrist. I was prescribed Librium, and my dad was deemed a half an inch from total insanity."

My mother wore the pants in the family. People would make fun of my dad and say that he wore lace panties. Dad tried to be fair, had a sense of humor, and more than once lost his temper because of my mother's hypocrisy. She was always jealous of others and would make comments like "How can they afford that!?" or "Who do they think they are?" and "They have no children, so they can have more money than they know what to do with." One would wonder why my mother even had children. She would always tell us her plans as to what she would do with our rooms when we were gone. Nothing like feeling loved and needed and respected. And my dad would threaten to shoot us all in our sleep, just to please her. My mother knew how to make people almost "chew nails"! I knew I gritted my teeth in my sleep for years. Nerves.

My mother would take us to church. It was a Methodist church where they preached hellfire and damnation. At one point, I literally had the hell scared out of me. I would come to learn Southern terminology of "getting saved" or "born again" many years later.

My Sunday school teacher, Mrs. Amisiger (in this Methodist church), introduced me to Jesus; and I found unconditional love for the first time when I was about nine years old. I was so taken with the fact that Jesus would love me no matter what. That is when I heard God ask me, "Are you sure?" I pledged my life for him through the old hymn "Are ye able, said the Master, to be crucified with me? Yea the sturdy dreamers answered to the cross we follow thee... Our hearts are able, our spirits are thine. Remold and make them, like thee divine." I still have the little book that I wrote the song in, in my Bible.

I had no idea what I was getting into, but I know God is with me and has always been there no matter what. My testimony is my proof.

I tell people that I was raised Methodist and Hypocrite, and I do not affiliate with either one of those denominations.

God is not a religion. He is a relationship. He has many names, such as the following:

Abba Father
Everlasting Father
Potter
Almighty
Creator
I Am
Most High

One of God's names *is not* Horton, but just think, in comparison, *Horton Hears a Who* (by Dr. Seuss), who lived in Whoville, on a teeny-tiny dust mote. We are comparable to the vastness of space; and God hears every word we speak, knows every breath we take, and even puts the desires of our heart within our hearts. I know for a fact this is true: "For it is God who works in you to will and to act in order to fulfill his good purpose" (Phil. 2:13 NIV). This is a confirmation of his plan.

When was that moment you first discovered "awareness"? That moment when you realized that you were not here by accident or coincidence but that you actually are a part of a bigger plan and asked, "What am I here for?" Look into the night sky and tell me there is not a bigger plan going on. One should stop and ponder, "You alone are the LORD. You have made the heavens, The heaven of heavens with all their host, The earth and all that is on it, The seas and all that is in them You give life to all of them *And the heavenly host bows down before You*" (Neh. 9:6; emphasis mine).

I started out with what I knew and had, to help God with the fact that time was running out and I wanted to be a part of the solution and not the problem. In school, I was aware of a girl who rode our bus. She was very poor, and I knew she did not have a lot of what I had. So I brought her home with me one day and allowed her to take a bath in our tub. She was always looking like Pig-Pen in the *Peanuts* comic strip. It took her two baths to get clean. Then I shared my slightly used clothes and underwear with her. She had no bras or decent panties.

Later, another girl would come to me and ask me to help her. When I entered her home, I was met with two feet of clothing on the floor throughout the house with animal feces mixed in all of it. The stench was breath-holding! Her mother was ironing, a thing she did to try to bring in extra money. A young toddler was sitting in the middle of all of this mess and was also very dirty and had a runny nose. As we climbed the stairs to her room, we had to risk falling as we sidestepped all the debris on the stairs.

We cleaned her room and hauled out three thirty-gallon bags of trash. Later, she would have the state emancipate her to a foster home.

Because of the racial riots in the late '6, our remote little town, in Bellaire, Michigan, was a safe place for exchange students, so…

We had four exchange students in our senior class. One of them lived with a fellow student until they had a falling-out. He then went to live with our high school counselor.

I was "in love" with Mr. Nethercot, our high school's first counselor. I had heard the other kids talking about how he had helped them find out who they were. So one day, I decided to make an appointment to see him as well. When I walked into his office and he asked me why I was there, I said, "I want to find out who I am." He said, "What is wrong with you just being you?"

Gee! I'd never thought about that! What was wrong with me… just being me? I told him the story of my home life and about my sister and was as forthright as I could be. I wanted the truth. He told me that my sister knew exactly what she was doing and that I was only defending myself the only way I knew how. He also told me, "You are like a breath of spring air!" I was in love. As far as I knew, he was the first person to let me be me and accepted me.

Anyway, when this one exchange student had a falling-out with his sponsored foster family, he ended up living with Mr. Nethercot.

I babysat for Mr. Nethercot, and one day while I was over there, I got up the nerve to tell Mr. Nethercot that this student acted like he liked me but at the same time acted as if I had the plague. I also asked him why that student treated me like that.

Mr. Nethercot said, "I don't know. Why don't you ask him?" I hadn't thought of that either. But I did, and this is what he said: "I had been told that you were not fit to be seen with." That really hurt because I had no friends to begin with! I did have two girlfriends whom I could talk to, but they were outcasts as well. The other kids called one Moose; and the other, years later, would confide in me, "I wanted to help you, but I had my own demons to deal with." It would be this one whom God told me to tell something to, as a witness that it actually happened later on.

When one of the cliques at school would drop one of their popular girls or have a falling-out, I would go to that girl and try to befriend her and encourage her, until she was accepted back into the clique.

Our family was poor, but I didn't know it. Living in the country made it hard to socialize because we were so far away from everyone who lived in town. But that didn't stop me from volunteering for things like decorating the hall they selected for our senior prom, even though I was not invited. I tried to fit in, but it was like God was holding me back. He had bigger plans for me. He'd given me a gift (mercy) that I was using and didn't know about until much later.

Evil never changes. Like I said, I was bullied in school, and there were days I would come home from riding on the bus and pray that God would end my life. Kids are still bullied to this day with dire results. We hear about it all the time with school shootings. Children today take their own lives at the age of ten, younger than ever. *Someone* needs to spread the word that they are not alone. We have an alliance in the spirit world that is watching over us. I guess I learned this at an early age and never once chose drugs or alcohol as a crutch. I had a lot of tears and suicidal thoughts, but I knew I had angels with me. And my family (after I was married) had entertained them along the way.

At the end of my senior year, in government class, I was musing about not having found anyone to love me and that I would soon be out in the big world not knowing any love or what to do. I was pining over a particular boy when God told me, "You don't want him. I'm going to take him home early." The mere thought of this frightened me, but then I said to God, "You're right. I don't want to be in love with someone that won't be there for me for life."

"And besides, someday," God continued, "he will tell you he's sorry for all that he's done to you."

That's when I told my other friend, Irene, what God had told me so that one day I could tell her that God's word came true. God told me to tell someone so I would have a witness. That someone is Irene.

Just before our twentieth class reunion, this young man called me and apologized for everything he'd ever said and done to me. I told him that I had forgiven him already but that he had really hurt me.

"I loved you," I said.

He replied, "I know."

Just before our twenty-fifth reunion, he was killed in a freak car accident. God took him home early.

Mr. Nethercot told me he wanted me to go to college. He said, "I don't care if you take a general course or flunk out! You need to get out of this town and know that there are people that will like you for who you are!" I did take his advice. I took a general course, and I was on probation. Hmmmm…powerful words had been spoken.

I graduated in 1968, but I did not turn eighteen until August. I started college that fall but dropped out after one term because…

I got pregnant when I was eighteen. I decided at the age of nineteen (1969) that I would give the baby up for adoption. My mother said, "You made your bed. Now lie in it." My mother had a spirit of spite and bitterness. She was the meaning of her name, Marilyn. My dad said nothing. But he told someone once that whenever he would see a young girl, he wondered if that was his granddaughter. He was in pain for losing a granddaughter.

I knew, in those days (the 1950s and '60s), I was *used goods*, and I was not going to let my child grow up with the stigma that had been attached to me through lack of knowledge and evil gossip. Mr. Nethercot said that if I had truly been a "bad" girl, I would not have gotten caught, and I would have not gotten pregnant because I would have been smart enough to use precaution.

When I was asked if I wanted an abortion, I said, "NO! That's murder!" I gave my child up. God gave me wisdom and strength to let go of another human. It was then that I learned we do no "own" another person. A child is a gift from God, and all I wanted to do was give that child a decent home, one that I knew I was not capable of providing in more ways than one at that time.

When one wants and needs to be loved so much, one will sometimes believe that giving in to everyone will make that happen, including having sex. I was never told I was special and that I should save myself for marriage. I try to teach my granddaughters (now) and my children (in the past) to respect another person's sacredness.

God created a hymen in the woman's vagina for a reason. When that is broken, she has made a blood covenant with that man *for life.* This is why remaining a virgin in some religions is so vital to their beliefs, in the Jewish faith especially. And, until Jesus died on the cross and shed his blood, animal sacrifices were to be made. The blood of Jesus changed everything. He made a blood covenant with all of those who chose to believe. In the book *Placebo*, by Howard Pittman, when he asks the demons why they hate the blood of Jesus, they reply, "Because it is alive."

I heard this testimony many years ago and do not remember from whence it came, but *they* vowed it was a true story. There was a woman who was as happy as she could be, until one day, for no apparent reason, she tried to commit suicide. For a time everyone was concerned, but as time went on, she seemed fine. Then it happened again. This time she almost succeeded and had to be hospitalized. Her friends and family were beyond concerned, for this was so far away from her character. Then one day they read in the paper where a man had committed suicide. To make a long story even longer, this man was the boyfriend of this same woman. She had a relationship with him many years before and had lost her virginity to him. She shared a *bondage* with this man because of a blood covenant. After this man whom she had made a blood covenant with, and forgotten all about, was dead, she no longer had the urge, ever again, to commit suicide.

* * * * *

Because in those days (the 1960s) I considered myself as "marked" used goods, I sat upon my bed in my room and told God that I would never be loved. That's when God spoke to me again and actually showed me a vision of my husband to be. I saw his head and where his face should be. It was as if a cutout had been made like a paper doll. I saw the way he wore his hair, and I told God that I wanted him to have blue eyes. (They were very patriotic most of the time: red, white, and blue). God told me that he was married and had a family.

I said, "But, God, isn't that adultery or..." I couldn't bring myself to say, but I thought, *What if they are killed?* I did not want to go there. This was in 1969.

In 1972, I met my husband, Jim.

We were both married to other people, and God's plan was about to unfold. Since I was married to a man who (I knew I'd made a mistake to begin with but couldn't say no, simple as that and stupid too LOL) was going to be a professional student, one of us had to get a job, and that was me.

Jim had moved up to Michigan and married the woman with five daughters from a previous marriage. She was the jealous type. One day she put a shotgun to his head and threatened to kill him for not agreeing to go along with what she and her family thought he should be doing. He grabbed the gun; it cut her in the place between her thumb and index finger. The law was called. They threatened to take Jim to jail. He held a gun on them and told them what happened, moved out, and started living with a coworker. I left my mama's boy of a husband and rented a bedroom with kitchen privileges from another coworker at the same place Jim worked.

Production was going slow for the legal mafia-owned (but Jim didn't know it at the time) factory. After all, he was just a hardworking guy from Tennessee loading the trucks on the docks. One day, there was a meeting, and Jim asked if he could give an opinion as to how things should go. They approved, and just like that, he was promoted to supervisor of the whole plant. He treated people with respect, let us so-called bodies have fans and music, and fired all the ones who were unreasonable with their treatment of the bodies. That is what management called us. In short, Jim got production going six months in advance.

In the meantime, I had been venting to my boss about my situation, and he told me that he rode to work with this guy, and we sounded like we were meant for each other.

When I dared to speak to Jim for the first time, I told him, "If I had a man like you, I'd treat him like a king and would want to have your babies." I had no idea, until we compared notes later, that the Jim God had told me I would marry and had a wife and family was *this* Jim! What God had told me in my early life had come true.

I only stayed with my new rental, a coworker from work, when she told on me; and that was a no-no. We, the bodies, were not allowed to socialize with the upper supervisors. Jim told me to stop working and that he would take care of me, and that way no one would be able to say we were socializing and breaking rules. We moved in with another couple and two weeks later got our own place.

Before Jim moved to Michigan and married his second wife, he had been living in Florida, going to college, and finishing up fixing to go back to Tennessee with his family. His wife and three children would go on ahead, and he would join them after he'd taken his tests. However, a Mr. Godwin, who was a deacon in the church where they had been worshipping and was also a neighbor, stayed up late one night, waiting for Jim to come home. He had a message for him.

Mr. Godwin had an interesting background. His parents had died when he was quite young, leaving him to be raised in a lumberjack camp. How he got there I don't remember the details or if they were even told to me. But he didn't even see a town (civilization) until he was in his twenties and did not know how to read or write. He married, and his wife would read him the Bible until one day she grew tired of it and told him he needed to learn how to read. So he prayed to God and asked God to please let him be able to read the Bible. Believe it or not, God answered and blessed him so that he could read the Bible, but not a word of the newspaper! He could also cross-reference things in the Bible. I guess that was one of the reasons he was a deacon in his church.

So Mr. Godwin came to Jim in the wee hours of that morning, with a message: "Do not let your family go back to Tennessee! I have had a vision or a nightmare. I'm not sure. Just don't let them go back! In this vision, there are five of you. But soon, there will only be two. And then you will walk alone. And then there will be five of you, but only four of you holding the pillars. I don't know what it means! Just don't let your family go back to Knoxville."

They went back. Jim got the call. My stepdaughter Myra, the middle child, remembered the night before. "I was fighting with my little brother, Blake, over a tricycle, when I heard a voice tell me to 'let him have it—it will be the last time he will play with it." It scared her, but she obeyed that voice. The next day when the phone rang at her grandparents' home, she started screaming and crying, "They're dead! They're dead!" Indeed they were.

They had been hit by a drunk driver. Her mother and her older sister and her younger brother were all gone.

Apparently, Myra and her grandparents, or at least her grandparents, didn't like Jim very much, because they got legal custody of Myra and, as good grandparents do, spoiled her. She had divorced her dad, which in those days was a rare thing. He walked alone.

He did remarry, and that's when I met him. He had been living in Tennessee and came home to an empty house. Apparently, her wife got tired of him being on the road and went back to Michigan where she had family. Jim would spend time trying to work things out with her, but when she threatened him with a shotgun, and it did go off and hit the head board, he left.

After Jim and I moved to Tennessee, some time had passed when I decided I should contact Mr. Nethercot and inform him that I had at last found true happiness. That only lasted from 1973 until 1986.

Mr. Nethercot wanted me to find some friends of his in Knoxville and associate with them for the purposes of joining Amway. But God had other plans for me...

I was in my early twenties when God took me to hell. One morning, I woke up dead. I knew I was in hell. I *knew* I was dead and that I would be in this place for an eternity. I was in a dome-shaped room that was solid rock. The walls were glowing like burning embers of coal. The room was only about twelve feet in diameter and less than six feet high, and it was *solid*. In the middle of the room, on the rock floor, sat two beings. They each had a stick in their hand and were stirring a fire that was in between them, on the rock floor. They would show a very evil and sneering sort of grin. Somehow I *knew* they were going to be my tormentors and that I would be here forever, alone and in the dark. The walls were getting darker and darker. The fire that burns in hell does not put out any light.

My thoughts immediately went to *My choices are over, and I won't be able to write any letters to anyone in here!* And just as quickly I realized none would be able to come to me either! Then I really started to panic! I did not want to be here, yet... I sensed a presence behind me to my right. It was then that I came to. I was back in my body and in my bed and in my bedroom. But at the same time, God asked me, "What can you bring with you to prove that you are worthy to stay in heaven with me for eternity?" I did not have to answer that because simultaneously, God replied, "It's what you give away that you take with you." And then he added, "Life is like a dream. Everybody has a dream that is so real, and they hold something in their hand, and they think that if they hold on to that object, they will wake up with it."

When one has an experience like that, it changes one, and one does not care what people think. I was given another chance to live and choose.

1982

God's plans for me were school, and not the normal kind of school either. God's plans for me were not Amway, which Mr. Nethercot wanted me to become a member of. Instead, I met Joan T., the wife of one of Mr. Nethercot's friends, who belonged to a group of women called Women's Aglow. She introduced me to all of the members. These women, of Women's Aglow, were from different religions coming together, under one spirit—the Holy Spirit. We would meet in one lady's home for Bible study once a week, and then once a month we would have a meeting where there would be as many as a hundred or more women. Thus began my schooling for five years, the biblical number for grace.

There was one Bible study teacher whom I admired so much, I wanted to be like her "when I grew up." LOL. I still don't know what I want to be when I grow up. Beverly's stories were funny and very informative. She wasn't afraid to admit that she was not perfect and many times would tell testimonies of how God first showed her these things and continued to do so. She had been humbled as a child.

Beverly did not like me. I told God this, and he told me that I should give her time, that one day she would brag on me. He said, "She does not know your heart like I do." After five years of Bible study meetings and fellowshipping, Beverly did brag on me. "I've watched this foulmouthed woman turn into a beautiful daughter of God who will go far and teach the world about God's love." Maybe not verbatim, but she did prophesy over me, and it was from God.

I was in a Christian bookstore, and the people who ran the store were watching me as if I were a thief, so I asked Beverly, "Why do people treat me so bad? I make friends, and then they turn on me, and I have never done anything to hurt them!"

She replied, "You are a very strong light for God. You attract people to you, but once they get to know you, they find out your morals are so strong they cannot stay in your light. You expose their dirt. So when you're a light for God, you will attract bugs." I could live with that, sort of.

It was in 1986 when God told me, "You need to get out into the world and share what you have learned. You are like a soppy wet sponge, too full, and you need to share what you have learned."

Nope, not going. Did not want to! But God moves in mysterious ways. I wanted to continue to be a stay-at-home mom.

The story of a little old woman who lived in the woods all alone comes to mind at this point. One day, she came out onto her porch to pray to God for ten pounds of flour. "I thank you, Father God, for ten pounds of flour, in your son's holy name, Jesus Christ. Amen!" What she did not know was that there were two little stinkers (boys) hiding in the woods, listening. Well, they just thought that was ridiculous. How could God give her ten pounds of flour like that? They decided they were going to prove her wrong. They went into town and purchased each a five-pound bag of flour and took it back to her porch. The little old woman heard the commotion and came out to see what was going on as the boys scampered back into the woods to hide. "Oh, thank you, Father God, for the flour!" Then the two little boys ran from their hiding place and yelled, "God didn't do that! We did!" To which she replied, "Oh yes, he did. And he used two little devils to do it!"

God used the pharaoh to imprison Joseph, under false accusations.

God allowed Satan to test Job.

So maybe God used my husband to boot me out of the house. He had started a five-year-long affair. (My "friend" from the song "The Tennessee Waltz"). He came home from his job, which had kept him out of town for a week—and he would come home on the weekends—and told me that I needed to get out and get a job! This after he'd told me that the most important job I could have was to stay home and take care of our son Gabriel and daughter Stacey.

Okay, who was this man, and what have they done with his body!? My *gut* told me there was someone else, but my god kept my mouth shut. I prayed that day. I told God, "I don't know what is going on. He's not treating me very nice at all, and if you have to break his damn neck to get his attention, do it."

God told me to go into the bathroom and take a hot bath. "It will be like you are washing all your past away and being reborn, and while you're in there, give yourself a hot oil treatment to your hair." Little did I know I was anointing myself for my ministry. God said, "Be still and know I am God."

Oh, that wasn't all. While I was in the tub, I had the TV on in the kitchen, and the Bob Braun show was on. He came on and sang "Be Still and Know I Am God"! Talk about goose bumps in hot water!

If I were to have to get a job, then I was going to have to have a career, and I needed to find out what that was. I wanted to be able to afford a babysitter should my husband want to take me out on a date. He never did. He had started a five-year affair… "And while I was dancing the Tennessee waltz, my 'friend' stole my sweetheart away." Remember I mentioned earlier that I played the same 78 over and over. It was "The Tennessee Waltz." She did become my friend, but I had no idea she was having an affair with my husband. My friends would say, "Valerie, you're just not on that level, are you?" I was trying to live the will of God my entire marriage and trusting him to keep things in order. I had learned a long time ago that I was not in control of another human. I try to live by example. That simple, but not easy.

In 1986, I could feel in my spirit hatred and destruction from my step-mother-in-law, Hazel. She was a very backward and uneducated person, who was ten years younger than my husband's dad (my father-in-law). Her family did not like my husband, Jim.

Jim, even with his family, had a reputation of being "crazy," and no one ever wanted to "mess" with him. However, my step-mother-in-law's family (we call them people) always believed that Jim was after his dad's land and everything he owned and that if James, his dad, were to die before Hazel, Jim would throw Hazel out in the street and take everything from her. Gossip was abundant, and things had been heating up, and for some reason, I could feel it in my spirit. I could literally feel this woman trying to destroy me.

So one day, I said to God, "Father God, I know that as a Christian, I'm not supposed to have hard feelings towards this woman. And I know I am supposed to pray for her, but I don't know what to say!"

He replied, "Bless her."

I said, "By golly, you're right. Your word says, 'Bless those that persecute you!'" (Rom. 12:14). Then I said, through clenched teeth, "Bless her real, good Lord!" It was at this point I literally felt a release in my spirit, and then I said, "But I don't want anything bad to happen to her!" I knew that I had released her into a just god's hands. And he said, "You let me handle it!" It wasn't long after that; and she ended up falling, went into the hospital, and never came out. She died about a year later. But while she was in the hospital, God told me to go and anoint her with oil. I got persecuted for that because "She never wore a pair of pants in her life as if wearing pants were a ticket to get in or out of heaven!" I was told by James (my father-in-law). Okay, I wore pants all the time; and in the old South, with the Baptists' "religion," that's a no-no. But not wearing pants isn't going to get you in or out of heaven!

I truly believe that God sent me to the hospital for the anointing, for future spiritual warfare, because when I was at the funeral of Hazel's mother, and they were giving the eulogy, I could literally feel the gnashing of teeth in the spirit world for her mother's soul. And God did not want this woman, her daughter, to go through that same battle. When we were in high school and went to the Smithsonian Institute in Washington DC to see the Hope Diamond, the security (technology) was so profound, I could feel the humming in my ears. This feeling of gnashing of the teeth was similar to that—very strong.

The mortician that took care of Jim's family in the funeral home told Jim that he'd taken care of a lot of bodies and that he could tell the ones that were at rest and those that he wasn't quite so sure of. He assured Jim that his family was "at peace."

I don't have all the answers to these experiences that I've had. Four years later, I would find out, from my sister-in-law, that this woman (my mother-in-law) I had blessed was plotting to kill me. Joyce, my sister-in-law, was in awe that I had even gone out to the farm to visit them. I had no idea! She said that they were going to let us come into the living room after we'd knocked on the door, which was in the back of the house; and as we came into the living room, she would shoot me and then profess that they mistook me for a burglar and that they had been frightened. That would have been a big mistake on their part.

As I write this book, God continues to give me messages that I need to share along the way. Just recently, on Facebook (this is to again confirm this book and its message) there was a post about a Mr. Lloyd Glenn. He was on a flight when he got a call from home telling him there had been an accident at his home. His three-year-old son had been crushed by a garage door and killed. The miracle is Brian, his son, recovered and had a story to tell about how the "birdies" had come to help him and tell him that "the baby" (he) would be all right. They also told him that he had to come back to tell everybody about the "birdies," that everybody has them and they try to whisper to us, because they love us so much, to do the right things. He continued to tell his mommy that the "birdies" told him that he has a plan. "You have a plan too, Mommy. Daddy has a plan. We all have a plan, and we must live our plan and keep our promises."

This book is my promise to God. It won't go away, and it is bigger than me, and it must be told. I have always believed that a person is no better than their word. And I have always kept mine as far as I could. There have been less than two or three instances in which I have not been able to.

The very fact that I share this book, my testimony, is an accomplishment of faith—faith because I am still broke and have nothing. I don't want this to be about me but about how God uses all of us. It's not my goal to become rich from this, but I want it to be a best seller so that people will see how simple and how powerful God is, even with the simple things. God even cares about a sparrow falling from the sky and the lilies of the field:

> Are not two sparrows sold for a cent? And yet not one of them will fall to the ground apart from your Father. But the very hairs of your head are all numbered. So do not fear; you are more valuable than many sparrows. (Matt. 10:29–31)

Consider the lilies of the field, how they grow; they toil not, neither do they spin: and yet I say unto you, That even Solomon in all his glory was not arrayed like one of these. Wherefore, if God so clothe the grass of the field, which today is, and tomorrow is cast into the oven, shall he not much more clothe you, O ye of little faith? (Matt. 6:28–30)

In 1985, while attending a Women's Aglow meeting, where we had a guest speaker and more than a hundred ladies in attendance, I noticed a woman in the crowd whom I could barely look at. I thought she was so ugly! And then, because I knew God could hear what I was thinking, I apologized to God and said to myself, *I know God does not make ugly people. Why, she's probably even somebody's mother who has had children and nursed them.* And then she looked at me. After the meeting, she came up to me and said, "God must love you so much! Because when I looked at you, my whole chest filled up with love. You know, like when a mother nurses her children." I couldn't speak a word.

Again, I say, Jeremiah was not the only person God knew before he was formed in his mother's womb: "Before I formed thee in the belly I knew thee; and before thou camest forth out of the womb I sanctified thee, [and] I ordained thee a prophet unto the nations" (Jer. 1:5). God knew all of us!

We are the meaning of our name. Our parents just think they name us; God is our name-giver, and he will give us a new name as well: "He who has an ear, let him hear what the Spirit says to the churches. To the one who is victorious, I will give the hidden manna. I will also give him a white stone inscribed with a new name, known only to the one who receives it" (Rev. 2:17). Again, I reiterate the kingdom of God is within each and every one us, and I will tell you how that ends later in this book.

In 1991, my friend Kathy Sawyer told me that I needed to know the meaning of my name. She gave me a plaque with my first name,

Valerie, on it. It means "strong spiritual purpose" or "determination." My middle name, Louise, means "battle maiden" (not battle-ax), or "victorious love." That "victorious love" confirms one of my spiritual gifts, the one that gets me into all kinds of trouble: mercy. I do not have it in me to hold hard feelings. I am not spiteful or vindictive. I believe God's words. I try to live by his words.

> And if someone forces you to go one mile, go with him two. (Matt. 5:41)

> If someone strikes you on one cheek, turn to him the other also. And if someone takes your cloak, do not withhold your tunic as well. (Luke 6:29)

> Do not avenge yourselves, beloved, but leave room for God's wrath. For it is written: "Vengeance is Mine; I will repay, says the Lord." On the contrary, "If your enemy is hungry, feed him; if he is thirsty, give him a drink. For in so doing, you will heap burning coals on his head." (Rev. 12:20)

Contrary to popular belief, heaping burning coals upon one's head is *not* a bad thing. In biblical days, if one ran out of coals, they would borrow coals from a neighbor and carry those coals in a clay oven on their head until they would get them to their home, thus saving a life.

I believe in Deuteronomy 32:35: "Vengeance is Mine; I will repay. In due time their foot will slip; for their day of disaster is near, and their doom is coming quickly."

God is the author of my reputation. He will and has vindicated me time and time again, as he will anyone! Knowing the meaning of my middle name, Louise, battle maiden, I decided to tell God that I was "battle-weary." Things in our home and relationship were just not progressing as I felt they should, given that I was trying to do the will of God every day and I wasn't getting a lot of support from my husband.

I was standing in our kitchen and looking out the window, to a large maple tree. Our property was surrounded by a highway that seven to ten thousand cars a day would pass by on the front side. Our house was an old farmhouse, and the acreage on either side of it had been sold off into subdivisions. I called it God's little acre. I didn't think a hummingbird would build a nest in a maple tree so close to so much traffic. I told God, "I am not trying to fleece you here, but I need a sign from you that you are going to give me the desires of my heart in this lifetime and not until I am with you in heaven. I know you give me the breath I breathe, and I know you put these desires in my heart! So would you please put a hummingbird's nest in this tree.!"

He then told me, "You don't want very much. You need to believe for bigger things."

Okay?

Two nights later, I went to a Bible study called More of Jesus, Less of Me. It was for weight loss. My friend Alora was sitting at the head of the table and speaking to one of the ladies on her right. I sat down on her left. As we waited for the other ladies to arrive, Alora continued to speak to the other lady. Then twice she looked at me and proceeded to continue to speak to the other lady, as if she had been unduly interrupted. The third time—apparently she had heard from God; he was the one interrupting her—she looked up and said, "Okay!" Then she turned to me and said, "God told me to tell you that you need to believe for bigger things."

Okay?

Two weeks later, we were sitting on the front porch of our home, with the cars buzzing by; and as I sat there, just a-swinging, this what looked like a giant beetle came flying from the far end of the porch and hit me in the head. I was sitting on the other end of the porch. I asked my ex, "What was that?"

He replied, "I don't know."

"It" came back and hovered between us as if to look us up and down. It was a hummingbird, and she had built a nest in that maple tree on the living room side of the house. The tree covered the whole end of the living room and kitchen side of the house.

I would watch her over the next few months diving at anything that would attempt to come near her nest. Then one day I decided that the branch was low enough that if I got a ladder, I would be able to see baby hummingbirds! I'd never seen any before. I got the ladder, and before I started up, I looked to see where Mom was. I did not want her coming at me with that beak! She was sitting in one of her favorite vantage points, cleaning herself! I climbed up the ladder and pulled the branch down and peered into the cutest two pairs of little hummingbird eyes—a boy and a girl. She wanted me to see her babies!

I still have that nest. It's in pieces because of all the moving I've had to do of late. And God continues to show me hummingbirds as a sign that he is keeping his promise. He even sent one to let us know that after Jim broke his neck and he had a spinal fluid leak for thirty-six hours, he would be okay.

Remember I had asked God to break Jim's neck to get his attention? In the fall of 1991, Jim fell and broke his neck. But Jim was a very stubborn man. I'm not sure that it got his attention at all because he started a second affair while in his rehab program of becoming a barber. He met another woman. This woman was friends with his first affair whom Jim had actually given away in marriage! My daughter was the bridesmaid, and it happened in our home!

Hey, I didn't write this soap. It's all part of God's plan whether one likes it or not, just like everyone's life is. We will all have our questions, and there will be answers. Until then, this is my testimony to help others become overcomers and let them know they are not alone.

When my son was still young, around ten or eleven (1986–1987), I encouraged him to become a Boy Scout. I became friends with the scout master, and apparently she liked the way I spoke about God. So when we had our summer camp, she asked me to give the sermon! I told God, "I have no idea what I'm going to preach on."

God told me, "Oh yes, you do. You've been playing with it for some time now."

I can't remember the exact thing I was playing with, but it was all about legions of devils can be wiped out with the army of God. Somewhere (but I'm not able to get to it at the moment) I still have that message. In the end, I gave the message that Sunday; and before I gave it, I went into the proverbial outhouse (literally) and prayed to God. "Please, dear God, just let me lead one little boy to the altar."

After the sermon, the whole room came forward, either to receive God or Jesus into their hearts, to get saved, or to rededicate their life to God. And as I stood at the door, like a real preacher, and shook people's hands, one man said, "I learned more in there than I did in six months in my church." Wow, I felt so humbled and blessed. God gets all the glory here.

Later, we would all sit in a circle and play the game where we started a whisper in one ear; and by the time it got all the way around the circle, we were amazed that it wasn't what was started at all! I told the boys, "This is why God hates gossip." I was using one of my spiritual gifts that I didn't even know I had (yet): teaching.

People will read this and ask, "Well, if you knew this, why didn't you?" and I will say, "Because my life is a lesson. Hindsight is twenty-twenty." And the gift of prophecy is only known in parts. God does not share all.

Through the years 1982–1985, we struggled financially. Not only did Jim lose his job from the factory he'd been employed with due to downsizing at that time, we'd also lost a water business that we had started due to the ones who started it. They had a drug problem, and they had sold us their water business called Blue Sky. In this business, one is assigned an area on a map as their territory, which means that area is where their leads or potential customers come from. But when the owners of the company take those leads for themselves because they are at the home office and intercept those leads and steal them from you, you cannot prosper. God sees all. Not only that, but the owner of the bank that we all did business with, Jake Butcher, went to jail for fraudulent practices. It's all documented in old newspaper files.

One day, Jim's dad came by flaunting a huge wad of money. He knew our situation, that Jim had lost his job and he was having a hard time finding a new career, and that only made matters worse. Jim's dad laughed an evil and mocking laugh, a "see what I've got here with all this money" kind of laugh, but he did give us a car to work on and sell. However, if one does not have money to buy toilet paper, one does not have money to buy the necessary car parts to fix the said vehicle. So the car sat in the alley for about eight months until one day…

Earlier, our son had found a box with three kittens in it in the park across from where we lived. We had a little dog, Freckles. If we were going to keep a cat, I would have to do some testing. I would allow the one kitten that Freckles would not growl at. I held each kitten up to Freckles. Only one got to stay; the rest went back into the park. We named her Lady Plush Bottom. She had a litter of kittens, and one day, one of them became quite lethargic, and we were afraid it would die. I told my son and daughter to put it back with its mother and to pray. The next morning, it was as if it had never been sick. My children had been taught the power of prayer and experienced results!

Not long after, on a Sunday evening, as we sat on our front porch, my nine-year-old son, knowing we needed money, apparently, had been praying for our situation. He came out onto the porch all excited and out of breath and said, "God just told me we were going to have two hundred dollars by tomorrow morning!" I must have looked like I didn't believe him, but only for an instant because he said, "You don't believe me, do you?" I quickly corrected and said, "If God told you that, then I believe."

It was about thirty minutes later, and this man came walking down the middle of the street appearing from seemingly nowhere and stopped in front of our house and said, "I want to buy that car."

My husband said, "I don't have the title to it," to which the stranger replied, "That doesn't matter. How much do you want for it?" My husband took this stranger to the alley and into the garage to get the battery. He had taken it out to prevent thieves from stealing the car. He told the stranger, "I'll take one hundred fifty for it." As they were standing inside the garage and the stranger waited for the battery to be retrieved, he looked around the garage and spotted a bed that we had stored there. "I need a bed," he said. "How much do you want for this?"

Jim said, "Fifty."

We got the two hundred dollars my son, Gabriel, had said God was going to give us. I, to this day, believe that the man was an angel sent by God to answer my son's prayer.

In 1987, I started nursing school, but not until I had gone through a program at Knoxville State Area Vocational School under Dr Luther Johnson.

Once again, God directed my path.

As I was driving along, I was looking for a secretarial college; and I kept being told, by God or my angels (because we all have them as well, and we need to use them), I needed to "turn in here" as I passed Knoxville State Area Vocational School. I went in and was directed to a woman whom I should have talked to last but talked to first, Mary Ann Piper. She would stay with me for a period of about a year and encourage me and give me the strength I needed to continue to grow in self-confidence.

She took me under her wing and gave me some advice that I needed to take this program. She helped me determine what my likes and abilities and other assets were to find out what program I needed to take. This is when I began an eight-week-long course under Dr. Luther Johnson. It was as if he'd been peeking in all our windows! He *knew* us!

Dr. Johnson and a colleague had, each, thirty years of private practice as psychiatrists and had come up with six types of personalities for each of us because of certain word phrases that they had heard over and over in the many years of therapy. They were so good at their analogies that NASA used them in their space program for compatibility with other astronauts they sent into space. One cannot get angry, walk out, and slam the door in space.

Six is interesting because that is the biblical number for man, according to Don Kistler's book *The Arithmetic of God*. This book contains the numbers of the Bible according to the authorized KJV (not the new modern translations) from 1 to 666, with infallible proofs from the Word of God revealing the meaning of each number.

Dr Luther Johnson came up with six types of characters. Six is the Biblical number for man. Since seven is the Biblical number for 'complete', I thought it would be meaningful for explaining that that if man asked Jesus into his heart, that would make seven characteristics instead of six, thus making 'man' complete.

Anyway, I learned a lot about myself and others in this eight-week study. I learned that my strengths and attributes were that I was warm, sensitive, and compassionate. Out of the six different types, I was a "reactor." These personality gifts that I had, according to the world's interpretation, would match up when I learned the hard way what my spiritual gifts were to a T.

There were five other personality types within each of us. It's like we live in this house (interesting…spirit in flesh), and we all have these different floors or personalities we go into at certain times in our lives, in order to cope, but our ground floor personality never changes. The other five types are workaholic, persister, promotor, dreamer, and rebel. I have been them all.

Dr. Johnson told me that I would make a good nurse. As he did, I looked behind me to make sure he was talking to me. He laughed and also said, "I learned never to laugh at a reactor when they put themselves down. They are the ones who need to be told more positive things more than anyone else because they've heard too many negative things, and it takes a long time to get over that." Robin Williams was a reactor-type personality.

I also learned that I was not crazy because as a reactor, we literally have the ability to walk into a room and feel the atmosphere and adjust to it. We are your empaths. We give what we need, and that's why everyone thinks we don't need what we give, but if we don't learn to overcome that weakness, we are the ones who commit suicide. We simply run out of what we never got and gave away. My strength is God, my faith. I thank God that I was wise enough to study his word and keep it in my heart and mind, and when I need it, it's there—*a truly living word.* It actually gives meaning to the moment when one needs it the most.

I also found out I wasn't crazy when I learned what my spiritual gifts were…later, at another painful "spot" on my path of life.

While attending this period of studying under Dr. Luther Johnson, I noticed that there were a lot of deaf people around. All of a sudden, I had an incredible urge to learn sign language. As I tried to learn, I would get flustered. They (the deaf) were very kind. I said, "I'm afraid my hands might say something they're not supposed to." They laughed and said, "Don't worry. We can read your lips better."

Little did I know I would later become the foster mother of a sixteen-year-old deaf girl. She would spend the night with my daughter. At first it was just a night. And then it became two, then three, and then she didn't want to go home. She actually would hide in my daughter's closet and not come out.

At the same time this little girl came into my life, another friend of my daughter's wanted to spend the night. She had an old-fashioned aunt who *coincidentally* worked with child services. When the deaf girl's mother tried to run her down with a car, I sought counsel and was told to get to Social Services fast, before the mother. As it turned out, I did get there just a few minutes ahead of the mother, so I was seen first. The case went to court, and for two years, I fostered this young woman. You see, she wasn't born deaf. Because of a cold that developed into an ear infection, which was ignored and left untreated by her parent, Misty went deaf. On her eighteenth birthday, through the aid of the state, she was able to hear again with a Cochlear ear implant.

While in nursing school, I made friends quite quickly and was surprised in doing so since I was so unpopular in high school. I had used some of the techniques I'd learned from Dr. Johnson to tell them about themselves. It was empowering, to say the least. But with newfound power came fear. I did not want to be in a negative popularity contest, and that's what it had turned into. So I ostracized myself from all of them, and then I was tested once again.

There was one student who was "crazy." No one knew just how crazy she was until the year was almost over. In the meantime, I was the "lucky one" to be put in clinicals with her and one other person. Just like all friendships, when there are three, one is usually a "crowd"—I was that crowd. I asked my instructor why she kept putting me with the same people. It was hard enough for me to try to concentrate and learn, let alone deal with high school games. My instructor was from the "old school," and she just thought if she kept "putting us in the same bag and shaking it up," we would all learn to get along. Well, the truth came out when this person told everyone that her little brother had died. When the faculty called the family to give their condolences, they learned that there had never been a little brother. The student was quickly dismissed from the program.

My instructor, Mrs. Jacobowski, had to publicly apologize and said she'd never seen such character.

I also had a patient in a Catholic hospital full of little nuns and a pastor. While wheeling this patient to his surgery, he was overcome with fear and wanted to make sure he was saved. I didn't hesitate in letting him know what to say and do. Later I would be reprimanded and told that they had a pastor for that sort of thing, and as I was brought before him, I asked him, "Who do you answer to?"

He replied, "God."

I said, "So do I!"

And then my head instructor told me that maybe I'd chosen the wrong profession, that what I had said wasn't the place for it. I replied, "Satan would have us believe there is no place for it." She remained silent, and I was allowed to continue my education as a nurse.

Going through all of this drama, again, I decided I wasn't going to work in a hospital. They were like small towns, and everybody "knew" everything about everybody, and I didn't need that again. So I became an agency nurse. I signed up with different agencies, and they would assign me jobs in hospitals where they needed an extra nurse. That way I was safe, and if they didn't like me and I didn't like them, I didn't have to go back.

I did everything—private duty, hospice, nursing home, and doctors' offices—and traveled a lot. But the steps of man (and woman) are ordered of God: "A man's heart plans his course, but the LORD determines his steps" (Prov. 16:9).

In 1991, I decided to stay put at St Mary's and was hired on the night shift (again to avoid drama) on the renal floor. Little did I know the head nurse had a reputation for being a tyrant. I'm so lucky... After a year, she called me her "little optimist." Because of her notorious reputation, one was never sure if we'd have enough help, and I would always say, "We will have more than enough." And we did. We got what I said.

I also had made friends with the young woman in the cafeteria who served our meals at midnight. One day, God told me to buy her a candle and to get a card to go with it. I asked God, "What do you want the card to say?"

He said, "You will know it when you see it."

I found the perfect one, I thought. It said, "Let your light shine."

When I gave her the card and the candle the next time I saw her, she started to cry. I asked, "What's wrong?"

She replied, "I had asked God for a sign. I wanted to be more like you, but I know they laugh at you and make fun of you." Goose Bumps City here.

Another time, God told me to go and speak with a patient who had been shot by her husband. It was a drive-by shooting, and to say the least, I was curious about seeing a gunshot wound. She let me see it, and I whistled. "What?" she asked.

I said, "I've never seen a gunshot wound before. At least it went clean through." And then I told her what God had told me to tell her. When I got done, she said, "You know, you said you didn't know me, but you just told me my whole life, and you're right." I have no idea what I told her, but it was for her and she received.

Again, I looked up and asked, "Why do you do this to me?"

1991

Remember when I told God that Jim wasn't being nice to me and that if he needed to break his neck he can do it? Well, Jim fell and broke his neck in the fall of 1991, a few months after God had sent me the sign I asked for—a hummingbird's nest in the tree outside our home. He had an affair during his rehab as a barber. His old woman, still angry with me, was friends with his new woman and had made friends with the young woman whom I had taken in to help escape from an abusive aunt. I can't make this stuff up. I'm a writer, but I deal with facts. I've always tried to use my imagination for much nicer things.

It was at this time—I had no idea—that my husband had been carrying on his affair for five years.

And again, I had opened my home to a young girl who claimed her aunt was abusing her. One day I caught her wrapping my photo album in a towel and going out the door with it. She was trying to hide it. I wondered why. When I saw the pictures they (it wasn't just her doing this), I asked her, "What are you doing with those pictures?" She said that Jim wanted copies of them because he missed our daughter.

I thought I had a rebellious teen on my hands when my daughter left our home for three months. I would find out that my husband had started another affair and was using our daughter to take care of this woman's children while they were "doing their thing."

What came next made me feel like I was in the friggin' twilight zone.

When my daughter was two years old, I had taken a picture of her naked, with her long hair that had never been cut. I also took a picture of her after with clothes on and her new haircut. When she was a little older, she came to me and was crying because she felt fat. I said, "We will take a picture of you now, naked, and later you will laugh at how skinny you are/were." Neither of these pictures were for nefarious reasons whatsoever. However, looking back and how they were used against me, I could understand how some would think the worst; and that is what happened...temporarily.

My husband had taken them to a preacher and told him that I had sexually abused my daughter with a lesbian friend of mine. Okay, someone's going crazy here, and just maybe it's me?

NO!

I asked God, "What do I do? Where do I go?" He told me to go to my friend Betty Anne Logan's house. She was like a mother to me (one of many of the women who were my friends, sisters in Christ, and mothers) from Women's Aglow. When I got to her house, she was on her way to a meeting for "women like me."

When we got to this meeting, it was about women who had been abused by their husbands; and Nancy Hoyt, Vice President Gore's advisor for family counsel, was there. I had no idea how big shots they were, and I was extremely upset and could not be still. I could not stop crying.

Betty Anne, being the old-fashioned decent Episcopalian that she was, said, "Now be discreet."

Oh he...no! I was being attacked spiritually big-time. There was no way I could be discreet, and so my whole story came out.

These two ladies who were at this meeting wanted to know how they could help me, because they could see I was visibly upset. One of them turned out to be Vice President Gore's advisor for family counsel, Nancy Hoyt.

The next thing I knew, the head of the Department of Human Services, in Knoxville, was offering me lawyers and anything else I needed. Talk about favor with God!

My husband made the mistake (he wanted to cover all areas) of wanting me to go to the church for counseling and meeting with the preacher, which I thought was unusual, to say the least. The preacher believed me. I told him that I was willing to come to him because I knew he was a true man of God and would be completely objective in his final opinion. But the preacher (Steve Fatow) did not believe me (fully) until he made us take these tests to let him know what he was dealing with. I came to find out, they were spiritual gift tests, and this would tell them exactly what and who they were dealing with.

This is when I found out that I had spiritual gifts! My main gift was mercy. I had three other ones as well: teaching, exhortation, and prophecy. So that's why I knew ahead of time things that were going to happen! God would tell me things, a gift of prophecy. I was not crazy!

My husband was going to try to build a case against me and send me packing back to Michigan, and he was going to get everything and have his new woman move into our home and have custody of the kids.

Needless to say, I turned down the offer from the Department of Human Services and just said, "I am in a spiritual battle here, and I need prayers and lots of them!"

But I did keep in touch with Nancy Hoyt. I did get my family back. But there would be more tests for me.

I had gone to work one day on a twelve-hour shift. This was in 1994. When I got home, I found a note from Jim saying that he needed time alone to think and not to bother trying to get in touch with him. Again, I did what God told me to do. I obeyed this letter, but I was devastated, and I prayed to God, "Where do I go!" He told me to go to Steve Fatow's church (we had gone to several churches over the years, trying to find the one that would give us the best spiritual food; Steve Fatow's teachings proved to offer more of truth than any other place), so I went.

I sat in the back of the church because I knew I couldn't stop crying, and I didn't want to make a scene. Then an angel was sent to me. This big, wonderful, and sweet black lady came to me and asked, "Wass the matter wit choo, honey?" I told her that I went to that church because God told me it was where I would find answers. She replied, "You're goin' wit me to Mona's!"

I had no idea who this Mona was, but I had the faith to believe it was what God wanted, so I left my car in the parking lot and went with this sweet stranger to Mona's.

Mona's was a house church, and it was there that for the next several years I went, and after I had gone just a couple of months, my family followed.

Mona married my daughter and her husband, and my son and his first wife. She and her husband, Dick, were the kind of pastors who were real. Mona was a prophet. God would tell her things to do, and she obeyed. One time, she and Dick went to the hospital to pray for a friend. When they got there, the nurse told them, "I'm afraid you're too late. He's passed away." That didn't stop Mona and Dick. They asked if they could still pray for him anyway. The nurse told them to "knock yourselves out." They prayed, and at 2 am, their friend got up out of the morgue and asked for his clothes. When the nurse told the doctor what happened, she got fired. He thought she was joking. Before this had happened, Mona told everyone that God was going to use someone to give them a much-needed vehicle. This man, their friend, was so grateful for their prayers, he gave them a "new" car; nevertheless, Mona's prophecy came true.

While I was there, Mona's daughter Rhonanda prophesied over me and said, "I don't know where you live, but it's like there's a light over your house, and everyone wants to come there!" This woman, Rhonanda, had no idea who I was, had never met me, but was spot-on. My family all looked at one another. I used to joke that the hobos, like in the old days, would leave their code of marks in our yard somewhere; and that's how all of these people, mostly children, would find their way here.

And when Jim left me for this other woman, I ran to Mona's at five thirty in the morning. It was raining, and I had just obeyed God and had come from where this other woman lived and confronted her and my husband.

When Jim was having an affair with the second woman, the phone rang one day. I answered it, and it was my daughter, Stacey. But I didn't try to beg her to come home. She asked to speak to her dad, so I gave him the phone. Then I heard him say, "Let me speak to Sta—," so I knew, but kept quiet, that he was still "seeing this woman." I don't remember exactly what day of the week that was (I think it was Wednesday), but Jim had been leaving very early to get to work. So on a rainy Saturday, a couple of days later, when he was getting ready for work, at a very early hour, I was told by God that I needed to follow him.

I said to God, "It's raining outside, and I don't want to go anywhere."

God replied, "You need to get dressed and make the bed and follow him. He needs to know that you know he is lying. Besides, you won't be able to sleep any way."

So I waited for him to leave. I got up and got dressed and went to where I knew this woman lived, and sure enough, there was Jim's truck. I went into the apartment building and knocked on the door. I heard her gasp as she peeked through the peephole and found out that it was me. I said, "Open the door and let me in or I will stand here and scream adulteress and knock so hard, I will wake the whole building." Needless to say, they let me in.

Jim said that I had no business being there. Well, I wouldn't be there if he hadn't been there. So I asked, "What are you going to do?"

He replied nonchalantly, "Well, I'm going to go to the farm and check on Stacey"—she had gone to stay with her Pappaw and Uncle since she couldn't stand being at this woman's house anymore—"and then I'm going to—"

I interrupted him, "What about our marriage?"

He replied, "I don't know."

I said, "I don't deserve this!"

He said, "I know…"

I was so upset that I went across the room and slapped this woman's face. How could he be so nonchalant about all of this! I wanted to slap Jim as well, but I thought, *Don't do it. He will hit you back*. I just knocked the cigarette he was smoking out of his mouth, but he hit me anyway. I fell back and hit my chin on a fish tank. And then I left to go out to the farm and wait for him. When he didn't show, I left and went to Mona's.

She said she would never forget that picture of me, standing there in the rain with blood on my chin. She invited me in and gave me hot tea, and then she gave me a picture of the Laughing Jesus, done by a personal friend, and said, "God is going to vindicate you, and everything is going to be all right."

Jim did come home to me a few days later, in 1994. Although he didn't cheat on me again, things still were not as they should be.

The young girl whom I had taken in to try to help, because she said her aunt was being abusive toward her, seduced my son. She was eighteen, and he was seventeen. She got pregnant. My son was working out of our driveway detailing cars to try to earn a living for them. Just before this young woman gave birth, she decided to call her dad and tell him that I had thrown her down the stairs, that I was abusing her. Lies…again.

Jim was gone. I had gone to work a twelve-hour shift, and when I got home, I found a note telling me that he needed time and not to try to contact him. Stacey, my daughter, had already been gone for about two and a half months (she was taking care of the children of my husband's woman while they did their thing). The young woman I adopted left; and my son, who thought he's in love with her, told me, "I love her, and that baby is mine, and I need to be with her to support my child."

Okay…

He left with his dad's credit card and very little money and a car that just *might* make it to Michigan and back. I prayed for angels to surround him and guide him.

He got lost in Detroit and stopped to ask for directions. He would later tell me, "Mom, this big, really tall black man came from the back of the room and asked me, 'You're not from here, are you, son?' and I told him no, but he came outside and stood there and pointed the way to where I should go and made sure I was safe!"

Then on the way home, he said, "She gave me an ultimatum, Mom. She said, 'Either stay here and never go back or go back and never come back.' And I saw where she lived and the conditions they were living in, and I'm a Southern boy, and I just couldn't live there! I had to come back! I stopped at a gas station because I was driving my poor car so fast. I was so mad, and the engine was getting hot, and the oil pressure was coming up, so I pulled into this gas station. I asked if they could use Dad's credit card, but they couldn't, and just then, this really tall man, who was trying to look like he was dirty for some reason, came into the gas station and asked where I'd been. Before I could tell him, he practically told me, and then he stopped like he didn't want me to know how he knew, and then he asked me where I was going. I told him Halls, and he said, 'I know some people in Halls. Always keep your eyes on God, son, and you will be fine. Why don't you go across the way and ask that gas station over there if they can help.' So I went over there, and they did, and they could. When I went back to tell them what had happened, Mom, that gas station was closed, and there was nobody there!"

Jim was gone. Stacey, my daughter, had been gone for almost three months; and now Gabe, my son, was gone. I wanted to commit suicide. I didn't know if I'd ever see any of them ever again, the ones whom I loved and had put all my life and love into. But instead, I went into my bedroom, and I sat down and talked with God. I said, "God, you are still God, and you are still on the throne, and I will get through this one second at a time"—strength came into me—"one minute at a time"—more strength—"one hour at a time, one week at a time, one month at a time."

He said, "I want you to go upstairs and clean your son's room from top to bottom and make the bed and turn the sheets down"

The next morning, at two o'clock, Gabriel came home and fell into bed.

Two weeks later, Jim came home for good, after I called Women's Aglow who were having a retreat in Gatlinburg and asked them to pray over my husband. I had at least three hundred women praying for me. A week later, Stacey came home. This was in 1994.

After a while, I felt that there was something different about Jim. I knew something had happened, so I asked him if God had been talking to him. Then he broke down and cried, something I'd rarely seen him do. He explained that one night, about two weeks before, he had been in bed praying to God. All of a sudden, there in the room were three angels! It frightened him, so he said he got up and ran into the living room, but they were already there! So he said he tried to run up the stairs (right next to our bedroom door), but he was unable to because of the density of the air. This made me recall the book *The Man Who Talked with Angels* by Roland S. Buck. In it, he said that when the angels would appear to him, the air would be so holy he was unable to stand in their presence. They told him to never worship them, only the Father and the Son, and that they would give him a type of "manna" to eat so he could stand.

Jim continued that when the angels first appeared, he looked over to see if I was awake. He said I was out cold, and therefore, he had no witnesses! He also explained that he felt very inappropriately dressed as the one in the middle was in a robe that was light blue and flowed with an unseen wind and that it was shimmering. Jim said there was a belt around the waist of the larger angel, and he *knew* it contained weapons of warfare. The angel raised his hand and said, "I am Gabriel. Be not afraid. God has heard your prayer." Jim said that when Gabriel would raise his arms, Jim could see up Gabriel's sleeve all the way into heaven.

About two to three weeks later, we had three miracles happen. The first miracle was our son, Gabriel, and his wife at the time were being sued for one hundred seventy-five thousand dollars. That suit was dropped. The second miracle was the mother of our grandson who was *stolen* for two years called and set up a meeting so that we were able to see our grandson for the first time since he was born. The third miracle was that Jim got approved for disability.

I would continue to go to Mona's house church, and Jim said he would join me when he was "good and ready."

Our family spent many Sundays with Mona and her husband, Dick. In fact, she married our son and his first wife, and my daughter and her husband.

But as the years went by, Jim would never stand up for me or support me, and everything that went wrong was my fault. Something had to change, and I knew I couldn't change anybody, so it had to be me.

One day in 1996, I woke up with a realization: all the years of my mother's abuse, and all the years Jim had not supported me, it all became clear—I'd married my mother! There's a saying that goes like "One marries a parent and becomes the other." I was so much like my dad, laid-back, easygoing, not wanting to roil the waters and make the storm any worse than it was. So for the next five years, I had to find a way to find myself and my purpose.

I made friends with my mother-in-law (Jim's birth mother); now very good friends, we went to the grocery store and to the movies. I wanted to let her know I loved her even though when she first met me, she had no idea who I was or what I was all about. I just wanted to be me as much as I could be, still doing what I could with what I had. But I had not gotten any support back. I was empty. She saw this and told me, "He"—her son, Jim—"still is not treating you right."

I had lost myself in my marriage and to my family. I had to build myself up and find my worth. I had the support of my father-in-law and my mother-in-law. I would not find out about my father-in-law's support until years later. He told me, "I told Jim I would pay for your damn lawyer!" He didn't like what his son was doing to me. Jim's brother, Jerry, who we would later have to identify by a tattoo on his hand, because he had been murdered and the dogs had eaten his face off, told Jim that "I will not lie for you."

Two weeks before they found Jerry's body, we had all gathered at Jim's dad's farm for a cookout. I was sitting on the picnic table when God told me to go over and hug Jerry and tell him how much he loved him. I couldn't and didn't. My butt just wouldn't leave the table. I *knew* that I would be telling him goodbye, and I just couldn't do it. I have had to repent for that.

Jim's very own mother, bless her heart, was eighty-three when she told me she'd help me beat her son up!

With all the negative aspects going on around me, and me being able to sense all of these things, I began to develop a lot of pain in my body. Again, I sought help and took yet another course to determine my abilities, likes, and opportunities to connect with my new debilitating health issues. I was diagnosed with fibromyalgia and depression. This testing was to determine if I should go on disability, which I *did not want to do*!

While I was going through this testing, there was one other person there with me. She had a funny way of speaking, and I couldn't help but wonder what her condition was, so I asked, "Do you have cerebral palsy?"

She replied, "No, I was in an accident, and I have a brain injury."

I finished my testing and was leaving the clinic, never to return, when I saw business cards for this testing. I was then told by God, "Take one." I thought, *No. Why should I take one? This is over, and I don't need to take one.* But then again, I heard, "Take it anyway!" So I did.

While taking an antidepressant, one must see a psychologist and a psychiatrist to determine if the medicine is doing its proper treatment. With HMO (Health Maintenance Organization), there are certain protocols for doing so, with insurance paying. After a time of one-on-one counseling, one must then go to group therapy. Yippee ki-yay-oh! This was something I did not want to do but had to, so again I went. The first time there were over twenty people there, and it was kind of interesting. The second time was a bit harder to convince myself I was going back, and I was good at talking myself out of it. *Who wants to hear my sob story?*

God said, "Just because you don't feel like you need this doesn't mean someone else does." Okay, I went back. This time there was only one other person there, and by coincidence, the psychologist had been held up by a phone call. So this other person and I got to talking. I mean why not? She told me it was the first time that she's driving a car by herself, "past the area where I had an accident." She too had a funny way of talking, and so I had to ask, "What happened?"

She replied, "I have a brain injury, and I need to find a place that will help me get tested to find out what I am capable of doing now." I reached in my wallet and said, "I think this card is for you." I had been carrying that card for over a year.

It took me five years to leave Jim. I decided to go back to Michigan and "find myself" while living with my dad. Five is the biblical number for grace. I even took a self-passed computer class in order to keep up with technology and my education. I also decided to get in shape by working out at Lady's Choice Fitness. I was gaining self-confidence.

I had a chance to go back to Michigan in the winter of 2001 to help my dad take care of my mother.

When we were growing up, my mother had worked at a nearby nursing home. One day she came home crying and said, "If anything ever happens to me, don't let me end up in a place like that." I told her she wouldn't have to, and I kept my promise.

In the fall of 2001, the doctors had diagnosed my mother with progressive bulbar palsy syndrome, comparable to Lou Gehrig's disease. They gave her six months, and that's how much she lasted. If someone did not come home to take care of her, she would have to go from the hospital into a nursing home.

I came home to take care of her instead of letting her go into a nursing home. I stayed from December to January and then came back to Tennessee.

While I was there though, I fell in love with my ex-brother-in-law and decided I was coming back for good in June 2002. He had made me feel like I was alive and appreciated as the woman I needed to be. Andy (not his real name) and I had been friends since second grade, and I knew that he had a crush on me in high school. We had always been friends. One never truly knows one until one lives with that person.

We divorced in 2016. He would not work, and the income we both received from social security was not enough to live on. Also, I made up my mind that it was better to live alone than be abused any more. Sometimes people do not manipulate by *doing things*, but by *not* doing what they are supposed to do. God did not tell me to marry Andy. This too was a mistake, but I didn't want to just live in sin either—not being married.

I divorced him because 1 Timothy 5:8 (KJV) states, "But if any provide not for his own, and especially for those of his own house, he hath denied the faith, and is worse than an infidel." I went on to get a job. He would not; and I truly believe it is the husband's role as head of household, according to the Bible, to be the main provider. However, he'd also proven to me that his needs came before mine, and they were more expensive as well.

I have to tell you this little incident because of another situation. One day while driving down the road to work, I was telling

God that it had been a while since I had found any money. I find pennies and dimes and change all time. I've even found forty dollars once, a five one time, and a twenty! So I was saying, "I'd sure like to find another twenty." All of a sudden, a louder-than-usual voice said, "Why not a fifty?"

I replied, "Yeah! I'd even like to find a one-thousand-dollar bill, if they even made them." The next night I went to the casino, and I saw about sixteen one-thousand-dollar bills. Yep, they made them. But this was on a Thursday when I was talking to God about finding money. On that following Saturday, I went to a grocery store; and as I was walking toward the cashiers to check out, I saw something on the floor, near the deli. Could it be?

I picked it up, and lo and behold, there was a fifty-dollar bill!

After I divorced my third husband in 2016, I got to stay in our house until it sold. And then I had no money and no place to go. So I called a friend, Jamie, and asked if I could stay with her. She said yes. I had allowed her to live with us at one time, and she was the one who told me why I was fired from my one job, four years after the fact. She had been a CENA at Meadowbrook Nursing Home in Bellaire. I was an LPN, but only for three weeks. Someone lied and told the head nurse that I was stealing drugs. Jamie told me that was why. I never knew until then, but I told God (when I was fired) I must have done what he wanted me to do while I was there, and I knew he would provide. I was devastated and humiliated and never even had the chance to defend (or know why) myself.

January 2018

I was homeless. And again, God provided. I stayed with a friend for a few months, and then when I had to move from there, a complete stranger, my boss from work, offered me her home for the next five months. God was with me. From there, I spent two weeks with my sister before I moved back to Tennessee to help take care of my daughter while my son-in-law would go on the road for his job as a tower dog.

While there, I had to get a new doctor since I was relocating. I was still on an antidepressant and needed refills. While at the doctor's, again I had to speak with a psychologist. He asked me if I heard voices, to which I replied with the story of the fifty-dollar bill. Then I asked him, "Do you think I hear voices?" No comment.

February 2019

That only lasted less than a year, and I had to move to where I am now. Still homeless, but God was in it all the way. I ended up staying with a friend that I had met way back in 1971. I called a friend whom I have known since 1972. She'd given me a key chain that says on the back, "This is the day the Lord hath made. We shall rejoice and be glad in it." I have never used another key chain. I still use it till this very day. Lynne and her husband, Clint, let me move in with them in Ludington, Michigan. I also got the only position they had in Walmart, the same one that I had in Knoxville, and went right to work without a hitch. Even the woman who gave me a hardship transfer from my job with Walmart was named Angel.

Every day God would send people, who actually listened to my story and told me that God would not leave me alone through it. I was happy with this job, and I made some very good friends. I even had a boss, Amanda, who liked me and was on the same page with me. I didn't have to worry about losing my job. Amanda was very fair and pleasant to work with. I could feel God with me like no other time, but I was not happy at all. I even tried to find a man on these online dating services, but nothing would happen!

I still felt very much alone. This was not where I wanted to be. This was not home, and I prayed to God daily to please let me go back to Tennessee so I could live in Morristown near my son, Gabriel.

While in Tennessee, before I had to "flee" to Michigan, I had been working with the University of Tennessee through Kelly

Services, cleaning the Alumni Building on campus. I made two very dear friends while there.

One, Cindy, said that she believed that God had sent me to help her. We are still friends, and I do pray for her and would do anything that I could to help her.

The other friend, Eric, was/is going through a trying time. One night, he wanted to call his son whom he had restraining orders against calling. I told him he should use my phone and to call him, that his son needed to know that he loved him and that he was doing all that he could to get back with them, him and his sister. The urge just would not leave me to tell Eric, and he finally called.

The other day, Eric called me and said that he *had* to share something with me. He said, "Do you remember that night that I wanted to call my son and you said you would let me use your phone?"

I said, "Yes."

He continued, "My son just told me that at that night, he was praying to God for me to call! I don't know how you do it, but just keep doing what you're doing!" Apparently I've also made an impression on his son. To God be the glory.

When I left my daughter and my granddaughter, and yes, my son-in-law, I had to leave them in God's hands. I didn't want to go anywhere, and I wasn't sure what I would face when I did arrive and whether I'd have a job in order to keep making the payments on my now-totaled car. But God said, "The bigger the fear, the bigger the blessings on the other side." So with faith, I went back to Ludington, Michigan, where I lived from February 2019 until July 2, 2019.

I felt like Joseph, Job, and now Jonah. I didn't want to be in the belly of a whale. LOL.

I wanted to be able to live in Tennessee and be near my son who helped me put two new tires on my car and fill my gas tank and put oil in the oil tank, just before I had to go to Michigan.

Now I will tell you how God talks to me and all of us.

The following scripture can be found in the Bible:

> Remember now thy Creator in the days of thy youth, while the evil days come not, nor the years draw nigh, when thou shalt say, I have no pleasure in them;
>
> While the sun, or the light, or the moon, or the stars, be not darkened, nor the clouds return after the rain:
>
> In the day when the keepers of the house shall tremble, and the strong men shall bow themselves, and the grinders cease because they are few, and those that look out of the windows be darkened,
>
> And the doors shall be shut in the streets, when the sound of the grinding is low, and he shall rise up at the voice of the bird, and all the daughters of musick shall be brought low;
>
> Also when they shall be afraid of that which is high, and fears shall be in the way, and the almond tree shall flourish, and the grasshopper shall be a burden, and desire shall fail: because man goeth to his long home, and the mourners go about the streets:
>
> Or ever the silver cord be loosed, or the golden bowl be broken, or the pitcher be broken at the fountain, or the wheel broken at the cistern.
>
> Then shall the dust return to the earth as it was: and the spirit shall return unto God who gave it. (Eccles. 12:1–7)

I'm not Joseph. But I can relate to him and all that he went through. As I have said, God put those stories in the Bible to teach us how he moves in mysterious ways. Joseph did not ask for what he went through, yet God was with him through it all, and in the end,

God used Joseph for his purpose. If Joseph kept a journal, I'm sure we would have heard all about his feelings, yet in a way, there was a "journal" kept. I wonder how many of our stories will be written down in another Bible. According to the Word of God, "All things are possible."

"For ever, O LORD, thy word is settled in heaven" (Ps. 119:89). The Holy Spirit watches over the Words of God. "For I am the LORD: I will speak, and the word that I shall speak shall come to pass; it shall be no more prolonged: for in your days, O rebellious house, will I say the word, and will perform it, saith the Lord GOD" (Ezek. 12:25). Jesus Christ stated, "Man shall not live by bread alone, but by every word that proceedeth out of the mouth of God" (Matt. 4:4). We will be judged by every word that has been recorded in these sixty-six books in this awesome volume of a perfect revelation.

And now, the crux of this book, *how God speaks to us*, how I knew in my spirit God was speaking to me through all my life's events.

Radio waves are one of the most important discoveries humans have ever made when it comes to our ability to communicate with one another. It allows us to speak through mobile phones, use Wi-Fi, and even watch television. When you turn on the radio in your vehicle, you're actually picking up radio waves that are in the air around you.

1. *They tickle electromagnetics.* Radio waves are often thought of as sound waves because they transmit sounds that can be heard. Over the radio, you can hear your favorite songs and sing along when you're stuck in traffic. In reality, radio waves are actually electromagnetic waves that are created when a magnetic field is joined with an electric field. These waves can travel very fast. They carry sounds but actually travel faster than the speed of sound.

2. There are many kinds of electromagnet waves that exist today, and they're all relatives of radio waves. Microwaves, sunlight, remote controls, radar systems,

and even Bluetooth technology all work because of electromagnetic waves. The difference in the radio wave is that the receiver of the waves can convert them into electrical signals, and then the radio circuit turns that signal into a sound wave. That's why you can hear someone talking through a radio, even if you're in the middle of nowhere (apecsec.org).

God's Word says, "Where can I go to escape Your Spirit? Where can I flee from Your presence? If I ascend to the heavens, You are there; if I make my bed in Sheol, You are there. If I rise on the wings of the dawn, if I settle by the farthest sea" (Ps. 139:7–9).

That's why one must live by every word that proceedeth out of the mouth of God.

We are connected, as I have said before. I have seen it, but it can only be seen in the spirit world, and there are very few who have had the privilege of seeing into the spirit world. I was blessed to be one.

What we perceive as our physical material world is really not physical or material at all. In fact, it is far from it. This has been proven time and time again by multiple Nobel Prize-winning physicists (among many other scientists around the world). One of them was Niels Bohr, a Danish physicist who made significant contributions to understanding atomic structure and quantum theory. According to him, "If quantum mechanics hasn't profoundly shocked you, you haven't understood it yet. Everything we call real is made of things that cannot be regarded as real."

At the turn of the nineteenth century, physicists started to explore the relationship between energy and the structure of matter. In doing so, the belief that a physical, Newtonian material universe that was at the very heart of scientific knowing was dropped, and the realization that matter is nothing but an illusion replaced it. Scientists began to recognize that everything in the universe is made out of energy (www.collective-evolution.com).

In Rebecca Brown's book *He Came to Set the Captives Free*, Rebecca tells the true story of a woman who served Satan, and while doing this, this would easily leave their bodies and wreak havoc upon people as if a poltergeist was doing these things. This evil woman said it was very easy to leave their bodies and travel to places and throw things around and destroy things; but when they approached a preacher's home to do the same, they were met with link angels, facing outward with their backs to the home, on perpetual guard duty. When they tried to throw things at them, all the angels had to do was look at them, and it sent them sprawling backward and helpless. It was at this time she realized there was something or someone stronger than Satan.

We need to follow a narrow path: "Enter through the *narrow gate*. For wide is the *gate and broad* is the *road* that leads to destruction, and many enter through it. But small is the gate and *narrow* the *road* that leads to life, and only a few find it" (Matt. 7:13–14; emphasis mine).

If we are outside of the will of God, we are not *living*. We are only existing. We have the ability to be like Jesus and perform miracles. We also need to know our gifts.

> Now concerning spiritual gifts, brethren, I would not have you ignorant.
>
> Ye know that ye were Gentiles, carried away unto these dumb idols, even as ye were led.
>
> Wherefore I give you to understand, that no man speaking by the Spirit of God calleth Jesus accursed: and that no man can say that Jesus is the Lord, but by the Holy Ghost.
>
> Now there are diversities of gifts, but the same Spirit.
>
> And there are differences of administrations, but the same Lord.
>
> And there are diversities of operations, but it is the same God which worketh all in all.

But the manifestation of the Spirit is given to every man to profit withal.

For to one is given by the Spirit the word of wisdom; to another the word of knowledge by the same Spirit;

To another faith by the same Spirit; to another the gifts of healing by the same Spirit;

To another the working of miracles; to another prophecy; to another discerning of spirits; to another divers kinds of tongues; to another the interpretation of tongues:

But all these worketh that one and the selfsame Spirit, dividing to every man severally as he will.

For as the body is one, and hath many members, and all the members of that one body, being many, are one body: so also is Christ.

For by one Spirit are we all baptized into one body, whether we be Jews or Gentiles, whether we be bond or free; and have been all made to drink into one Spirit.

For the body is not one member, but many.

If the foot shall say, Because I am not the hand, I am not of the body; is it therefore not of the body?

And if the ear shall say, Because I am not the eye, I am not of the body; is it therefore not of the body?

If the whole body were an eye, where were the hearing? If the whole were hearing, where were the smelling?

But now hath God set the members every one of them in the body, as it hath pleased him.

And if they were all one member, where were the body?

But now are they many members, yet but one body.

And the eye cannot say unto the hand, I have no need of thee: nor again the head to the feet, I have no need of you.

Nay, much more those members of the body, which seem to be more feeble, are necessary:

And those members of the body, which we think to be less honourable, upon these we bestow more abundant honour; and our uncomely parts have more abundant comeliness.

For our comely parts have no need: but God hath tempered the body together, having given more abundant honour to that part which lacked:

That there should be no schism in the body; but that the members should have the same care one for another.

And whether one member suffer, all the members suffer with it; or one member be honoured, all the members rejoice with it.

Now ye are the body of Christ, and members in particular.

And God hath set some in the church, first apostles, secondarily prophets, thirdly teachers, after that miracles, then gifts of healings, helps, governments, diversities of tongues.

Are all apostles? are all prophets? are all teachers? are all workers of miracles?

Have all the gifts of healing? do all speak with tongues? do all interpret?

But covet earnestly the best gifts: and yet shew I unto you a more excellent way. (1 Cor. 10–31 KJV)

Marilyn Hickey's book *Know Your Ministry* is a good reference to using one's spiritual gifts. As a nurse, I witnessed EKGs, MRIs, X-rays, tools that can pass through the human body unseen.

God wants to use us this way and can use us this way, every day, twenty-four seven, but what do we do? We give in to our five senses and miss the miracles.

We do not heed the unseen world, which is more permanent than this world: "A person who does not have the Spirit does not accept the truths that come from the Spirit of God. That person thinks they are foolish and cannot understand them, because they can only be judged to be true by the Spirit" (1 Cor. 2:14 New Century Version [NCV]).

All of us have had the feeling of intuition, or déjà vu. Most would agree that they have a conscience. What if that was God talking to you? Most know right from wrong. I have always said, and I truly believe this, that we have an angel sitting on one shoulder and a demon on the other. We listen to them to guide our life. To know the difference, one must know the instructions, the Word of God, the Bible.

Just recently, while tending to some customers, I heard them talking about a project they were making and having their mom help them. I interjected, "Yeah, let Mumsy help you!"

They replied, "That's what we call her." How did I know that? I had never met their mother, nor did I know this. We are connected.

There are waves of energy all around us. These things happen to me all the time. They happen to all us. We *need to tune in*.

I had told God, when I was very young, that he needed to speak to me in any way, shape, or form because I was "kinda slow," and I needed to hear from him. He speaks to me constantly. Although I am not perfect, never will be, I strive to be the best I can be for my Father in heaven. He knows my heart.

I know his voice because I am connected to him, and so are all of you, by an unseen umbilical cord.

When I was six or seven, in 1956–57, my mother made me take a nap. I was not sleepy, and I did not want to take a nap. But I had to, and then I was outside. Hey, I didn't have to take a nap, and I could play as I had wanted to. But as I leaned down to pick up something to play with, my hand went right through it! *This is not right! What is going on?* I looked back toward the front door of the house, and that's when I saw it.

The silver cord that is spoken of in Ecclesiastes! Commentaries refer to this as the spinal cord, but there is an unseen cord, only to be seen with spiritual eyes, and I have seen this. It is attached to our gut. Some would call it chakra. Since it was coming out of my back, I'd say it is in the vicinity of the heart.

In 2009, God told me to look up the conductivity of silver. I did, and I was surprised to find out that *it is the most conductive* material, not gold. And since our bodies are earthen, we contain all the earth's elements within us.

Composition of the human body

Body composition may be analyzed in various ways. This can be done in terms of the chemical elements present, or by molecular type e.g., water, protein, fats (or lipids), hydroxylapatite (in bones), carbohydrates (such as glycogen and glucose) and DNA. In terms of tissue type, the body may be analyzed into water, fat, connective tissue, muscle, bone, etc. In terms of cell type, the body contains hundreds of different types of cells, but notably, the largest number of cells contained in a human body (though not the largest mass of cells) are not human cells, but bacteria residing in the normal human gastrointestinal tract.

Contents

Elements

The main elements that compose the human body are shown from most abundant (by mass, not by fraction of atoms) to least abundant.

201 Elements of the Human Body.02.svg	Element Symbol	% in body
Oxygen	O	65.0
Carbon	C	18.5
Hydrogen	H	9.5
Nitrogen	N	3.2
Calcium	Ca	1.5
Phosphorus	P	1.0
Potassium	K	0.4
Sulfur	S	0.3
Sodium	Na	0.2
Chlorine	Cl	0.2
Magnesium	Mg	0.2
Others		< 1.0

Pie charts of typical human body composition by percent of mass, and by percent of atomic composition (atomic percent).

Almost 99% of the mass of the human body is made up of six elements: oxygen, carbon, hydrogen, nitrogen, calcium, and phosphorus. Only about 0.85% is composed of another five elements: potassium, sulfur, sodium, chlorine, and magnesium. All 11 are necessary for life. The remaining elements are trace elements, of which more than a dozen are thought on the basis of good evidence to be necessary for life. All of the mass of the trace elements put together (less than 10 grams for a human body) do not add up to the body mass of magnesium, the least common of the 11 non-trace elements.

Other elements

Not all elements which are found in the human body in trace quantities play a role in life. Some of these elements are thought to be simple bystander contaminants without function (examples: cesium, titanium), while many others are thought to be active toxics, depending on amount (cadmium, mercury, radioactive). The possible utility and toxicity of a few elements at levels normally found in the body (aluminum) is debated. Functions have been proposed for trace amounts of cadmium and lead, although these are almost certainly toxic in amounts very much larger than normally found in the body. There is evidence that arsenic, an element normally considered a toxin in higher amounts, is essential in ultratrace quantities, in mammals such as rats, hamsters, and goats.

Some elements (silicon, boron, nickel, vanadium) are probably needed by mammals also, but in far smaller doses. Bromine is used abundantly by some (though not all) lower organisms, and opportunistically in eosinophils in humans. One study has found bromine to be necessary to collagen IV synthesis in humans. Fluorine is used by a number of plants to manufacture toxins (see that element) but in humans only functions as a local (topical) hardening agent in tooth enamel, and not in an essential biological role.

Elemental composition list
Main article: mineral (nutrient)

The average 70 kg (150 lb) adult human body contains approximately 7×1027 atoms and contains at least detectable traces of 60 chemical elements. About 29 of these elements are thought to play an active positive role in life and health in humans.

The relative amounts of each element vary by individual, mainly due to differences in the proportion of fat, muscle and bone in their body. Persons with more fat will have a higher proportion of carbon and a lower proportion of most other elements (the proportion of hydrogen will be about the same). The numbers in the table are averages of different numbers reported by different references.

The adult human body averages ~53% water. This varies substantially by age, sex, and adiposity. In a large sample of adults of all ages and both sexes, the figure for water fraction by weight was found to be 48 ±6% for females and 58 ±8% water for males. Water is ~11% hydrogen by mass but ~67% hydrogen by atomic percent, and these numbers along with the comple-mentary % numbers for oxygen in water, are the largest contributors to overall mass and atomic composition figures. Because of water content, the human body contains more oxygen by mass than any other element, but more hydrogen by atom-fraction than any element.

The elements listed below as "Essential in humans" are those listed by the (US) Food and Drug Administration as essential nutrients, as well as six additional elements: oxygen, car-bon, hydrogen, and nitrogen (the fundamental building blocks of life on Earth), sulfur (essential to all cells) and cobalt (a necessary component of vitamin B12). Elements listed as "Possibly" or "Probably" essential are those cited by the National Research Council (United States) as beneficial to human health and possibly or prob-ably essential.

Atomic number	Element	Fraction of mass	Mass (kg)	Atomic percent	Essential in humans	Negative effects of excess	Group
8	Oxygen	0.65	43	24	Yes (e.g. water, electron acceptor)	Reactive oxygen species	16
6	Carbon	0.18	16	12	Yes (organic compounds)	14	
1	Hydrogen	0.10	7	62	Yes (e.g. water)	1	
7	Nitrogen	0.03	1.8	1.1	Yes (e.g. DNA and amino acids)	15	
20	Calcium	0.014	1.0	0.22	Yes (e.g. Calmodulin and Hydroxylapatite in bones)	2	
15	Phosphorus	0.011	0.78	0.22	Yes (e.g. DNA and phosphorylation)	white allotrope highly toxic	15
19	Potassium	2.0×10^{-3}	0.14	0.033	Yes (e.g. Na+/ K+-ATPase)	1	

16	Sulfur	2.5×10−3	0.14	0.038	Yes (e.g. Cysteine, Methionine, Biotin, Thiamine)	16
11	Sodium	1.5×10−3	0.10	0.037	Yes (e.g. Na+/K+-ATPase)	1
17	Chlorine	1.5×10−3	0.095	0.024	Yes (e.g. Cl-transporting ATPase)	17
12	Magnesium	500×10−6	0.019	0.0070	Yes (e.g. binding to ATP and other nucleotides)	2
26	Iron*	60×10−6	0.0042	0.00067	Yes (e.g. Hemoglobin, Cytochromes)	8
9	Fluorine	37×10−6	0.0026	0.0012	Yes (AUS, NZ), No (US, EU), Maybe (WHO) toxic in high amounts	17
30	Zinc	32×10−6	0.0023	0.00031	Yes (e.g. Zinc finger proteins)	12
14	Silicon	20×10−6	0.0010	0.0058	Possibly	14
37	Rubidium	4.6×10−6	0.00068	0.000033	No	1

38	Strontium	4.6×10^{-6}	0.00032	0.000033	—	2	
35	Bromine	2.9×10^{-6}	0.00026	0.000030	—	17	14
82	Lead	1.7×10^{-6}	0.00012	0.0000045	No	toxic	
29	Copper	1×10^{-6}	0.000072	0.0000104	Yes (e.g. copper proteins)	11	12
13	Aluminium	870×10^{-9}	0.000060	0.000015	No	13	
48	Cadmium	720×10^{-9}	0.000050	0.0000045	No	toxic	
58	Cerium	570×10^{-9}	0.000040	No	No		
56	Barium	310×10^{-9}	0.000022	0.0000012	No	toxic in higher amounts	2
50	Tin	240×10^{-9}	0.000020	6.0×10^{-7}	No	14	
53	Iodine	160×10^{-9}	0.000020	7.5×10^{-7}	Yes (e.g. thyroxine, triiodothyronine)	17	
22	Titanium	130×10^{-9}	0.000020	No	4		
5	Boron	690×10^{-9}	0.000018	0.0000030	Probably	13	
34	Selenium	190×10^{-9}	0.000015	4.5×10^{-8}	Yes	toxic in higher amounts	16

28	Nickel	140×10^{-9}	0.000015	0.0000015	Probably	toxic in higher amounts	10
24	Chromium	24×10^{-9}	0.000014	8.9×10^{-8}	Yes	6	
25	Manganese	170×10^{-9}	0.000012	0.0000015	Yes (e.g. Mn-SOD)	7	
33	Arsenic	260×10^{-9}	0.000007	8.9×10^{-8}	Possibly	toxic in higher amounts	15
3	Lithium	31×10^{-9}	0.000007	0.0000015	Yes (intercorrelated with the functions of several enzymes, hormones and vitamins)	toxic in higher amounts	1
80	Mercury	190×10^{-9}	0.000006	8.9×10^{-8}	No	toxic	12
55	Caesium	21×10^{-9}	0.000006	1.0×10^{-7}	No	1	
42	Molybdenum	130×10^{-9}	0.000005	4.5×10^{-8}	Yes (e.g. the molybdenum oxotransferases, Xanthine oxidase and Sulfite oxidase)	6	
32	Germanium	5×10^{-6}	No	14			

27	Cobalt	21×10−9	0.000003	3.0×10−7	Yes (cobalamin, B12)	9
51	Antimony	110×10−9	0.000002	No	toxic	15
47	*Silver*	*10×10−9*	*0.000002*	*No*	*11*	
41	Niobium	1600×10−9	0.0000015	No	5	4
40	Zirconium	6×10−6	0.000001	3.0×10−7	No	
57	Lanthanum	1370×10−9	8×10−7	No		
52	Tellurium	120×10−9	7×10−7	No	16	
31	Gallium	7×10−7	No	13		
39	Yttrium	6×10−7	No	3		
83	Bismuth	5×10−7	No	15		
81	Thallium	5×10−7	No	highly toxic	13	
49	Indium	4×10−7	No	13		
79	Gold	3×10−9	2×10−7	3.0×10−7	No	
					uncoated nanoparticles possibly genotoxic	11
21	Scandium	2×10−7	No	3		
73	Tantalum	2×10−7	No	5		

23	Vanadium	$260×10^{-9}$	$1.1×10^{-7}$	$1.2×10^{-8}$	Possibly (suggested osteo-metabolism (bone) growth factor) 5
90	Thorium	$1×10^{-7}$	No	toxic, radioactive	
92	Uranium	$1×10^{-7}$	$3.0×10^{-9}$	No	toxic, radioactive
62	Samarium	$5.0×10^{-8}$	No	No	
74	Tungsten	$2.0×10^{-8}$	No	6	
4	Beryllium	$3.6×10^{-8}$	$4.5×10^{-8}$	No	toxic in higher amounts 2
88	Radium	$3×10^{-14}$	$1×10^{-17}$	No	toxic, radioactive 2

*Iron = ~3 g in men, ~2.3 g in women

Of the 94 naturally occurring chemical elements, 60 are listed in the table above. Of the remaining 34, it is not known how many occur in the human body.

Most of the elements needed for life are relatively common in the Earth's crust. Aluminium, the third most common element in the Earth's crust (after oxygen and silicon), serves no function in living cells, but is harmful in large amounts. Transferrin's can bind aluminums.

Periodic table
Nutritional elements in the periodic table

```
H  He
Li Be  B   C   N   O   F   Ne
Na Mg  Al  Si  P   S   Cl  Ar
K  Ca Sc Ti  V  Cr Mn Fe  Co Ni Cu Zn Ga Ge As Se Br Kr
Rb Sr Y  Zr Nb Mo Tc Ru  Rh Pd Ag Cd In Sn Sb Te I  Xe
Cs Ba La *  Hf Ta W  Re  Os Ir Pt Au Hg Tl Pb Bi Po At Rn
Fr Ra Ac ** Rf Db Sg Bh  Hs Mt Ds Rg Cn Nh Fl Mc Lv Ts Og

*  Ce Pr Nd Pm Sm Eu Gd Tb Dy Ho Er Tm Yb Lu
** Th Pa U  Np Pu Am Cm Bk Cf Es Fm Md No Lr
```

The four basic organic elements
Quantity elements
Essential trace elements

Deemed essential trace element by U.S., not by European Union
    Suggested function from deprivation effects or active metabolic handling, but no clearly-identified biochemical function in humans
    Limited circumstantial evidence for trace benefits or biological action in mammals

No evidence for biological action in mammals, but essential in some lower organisms.

(In the case of lanthanum, the definition of an essential nutrient as being indispensable and irreplaceable is not completely applicable due to the extreme similarity of the lanthanides. Thus Ce, Pr, and Nd may be substituted for La without ill effects for organisms using La, and the smaller Sm, Eu, and Gd may also be similarly substituted but cause slower growth.). (wikipedia.org)

It was in 2009 when I discovered the silver cord in the Bible as well. Even though I had read the Bible from cover to cover, I had forgotten that I had read Ecclesiastes 12:6–7, which describes the final end of man: "Remember your Creator before the silver cord is loosed, or the golden bowl is broken, or the pitcher shattered at the fountain, or the wheel broken at the well."

When that silver cord is broken, our spirit goes back to God. *Notice the number 11 after silver...*

Promises, promises.

The gospel of John records *eleven* very special promises.

A person can receive everlasting life by believing in the Son of God (John 3:16).

A person can have eternal life by eating, spiritually, Jesus's body (John 6:54).

By following Jesus, you will not walk in darkness (John 8:12).

Those who continue in Jesus's word will be set free (John 8:31–32).

A person will truly be *free* if made so by Jesus (John 8:36).

God the Father will honor those who serve Christ (John 12:26).

Those who believe in Jesus will do greater deeds than he did (John 14:12).

Those who obey Christ's commands will receive the Holy Spirit (John 14:15–16).

Those who keep Jesus's commands will be loved by both him and God the Father (John 14:21).

Those who abide in Jesus will be fruitful (John 15:5).

The last of the eleven promises is that a person can be Christ's friend *if* they obey him (John 15:14) (www.biblestudy.org).

> Conductivity refers to the ability of a material to transmit energy. There are different types of conductivity, including electrical, thermal, and acoustical conductivity. The most electrically conductive element is silver, followed by copper and gold. Silver also has the highest thermal conductivity of any element and the highest light reflectance. Although it is the best conductor, copper and gold are used more often in electrical applications because copper is less expensive and gold has a much higher corrosion resistance. Because silver tarnishes, it is less desirable for high frequencies because the exterior surface becomes less conductive.
>
> As to why silver is the best conductor, the answer is that its electrons are freer to move than those of the other elements. This has to do with its valence and crystal structure.
>
> Most metals conduct electricity. Other elements with high electrical conductivity, are aluminum, zinc, nickel, iron, and platinum. Brass and bronze are electrically conductive alloys, rather than elements. (www.thoughtco.com)

The best conductor to move energy is silver! We human vessels are all energy.

God is energy. God is numbers. Numbers never change. God never changes. God is love. God sent his son—energy, numbers, love—to save us all.

There is only one truth.

It is God who speaks to all of us all the time.

Each and every single one of us needs to tune in to that frequency and listen.

As I write this book and open candy wrappers, even they speak to me. Don't stop until you're proud. Be the sculptor of your life. Be the one you look up to. I love Dove. LOL.

In my journal, since I have been homeless, God has spoken to me daily.

I am not alone.
We are not alone.
God still uses people today just as he did in biblical days.
Jacob was a liar.
Joseph was abused.
Moses had a stuttering problem.
Gideon was afraid.
Samson had long hair and was a womanizer.
Rahab was a prostitute.
Jeremiah and Timothy were too young.
David had an affair and was a murderer.
Elijah was suicidal.
Job went bankrupt.
Peter denied Christ.
The disciples all fell asleep when Jesus needed them most.
Martha worried too much about everything.
Zacchaeus was too small.
Lazarus was raised from the dead.
What's your excuse?

It's strange how the two friends that I made, while working at the University of Tennessee, Eric and Cindy, call me about the same time all the time. Weeks can go by, and then one day I will hear from one, and then I will hear from the other, and they are not aware of this. But I am. God does, and there's a reason we keep in touch. The last time I heard from both of them, prayers had been answered, for both of them! God made an impression within them using me, and I get to hear the blessings!

It feels good to be used by God. I have counted it all joy when I have suffered from persecutions.

> Consider it pure joy, my brothers, when you encounter trials of many kinds, because you know that the testing of your faith develops perseverance. (James 1:2–3)

> Rejoice and be glad, because great is your reward in heaven; for in the same way they persecuted the prophets before you. (Matt. 5:12)

When we say we don't sin because we don't lie or cheat or kill or steal, we still sin every single time we refuse to listen to that still small voice that is of God. When we go against his will, then we have consequences.

No one is perfect. No one can be. But if we try daily, minute by minute, hour by hour, God sees and will use us to do his will. And we will reap. When? In his timing, and his timing is always perfect.

Pray for God's wisdom. He will share. Pray for God's strength. He will share. He has plenty to give.

God does not care what color you are, how old you are, what you've done or not done. He does not care where you live or how much you have or don't have. All he cares about is your eternal soul, and *he loves you unconditionally.* As long as one has breath and that cord is attached, one has a choice for heaven or eternal hell.

Remember Ecclesiastes 12:6–7: we are connected to God whether we believe or not, and as long as that *cord* is there, we have a choice—a choice that is *eternal.*

I can look at all I see and "own" it because I am "aware." I do not have to take it home and literally own whatever I see, worry about how I am to pay for things or pay taxes, or even have things stolen from me. I am a very small part of God's creation and do not take up much space, and God meets all my basic needs. If he wants me to have more than that, he will provide. I believe that God keeps his promise to me for bigger things. Interpretation is in the eye of the beholder, and God only needs to prove to me his ultimate plan through this willing earthen vessel, no one else's.

EPILOGUE

My story is far from over. In fact, in many ways it's just begun, for the past is in the past and tomorrow is not here. We only have the present. As long as one has breath, one must live the plan.

It is now July 2019. God has answered my prayers. I am back in Tennessee with the father of my children, whom I get to see all the time now, along with my grandchildren. After all, isn't that what life is all about? Family.

But let me tell you just how big a miracle this is from my husband's point of view. He should have been dead long ago. Ten times the enemy tried to take him out before God's plan was fulfilled:

1945. Jim's mother was told he only had eight weeks to live because of Bright's Disease. Obviously he survived. He'd heard the doctor, and he made up his mind he was going to fight it, and he did.

1954. While out with a friend, Dan Whaley, riding motorcycles and driving into a curve at over 90 mph, Jim survived, but Dan did not. This was also a time when Jim was running moonshine, and when he went to the home of his friend to tell his uncle he was sorry for his loss, he was threatened with his life by two of Dan's friends with a gun. Jim, being as crazy as he was, while in his vehicle, jumped (over the lap of his wife, Mary Kay, on the passenger's side) out the window and jumped in their car with his hawkbill knife stabbing and hitting. They left him alone, until a couple of weeks later when Jim was summoned to a remote restaurant late at night. He waited for whoever told him to be there, and the owner of the restaurant told Jim that there were about nine cars outside (in the dark, with their headlights on) waiting to do him some serious harm. The owner wanted to know if he should call the police. "No," said Jim, "I'll handle this." So he went out, again with his hawkbill knife, and confronted grown men who were in the moonshine business and said, "Okay, there are a bunch of you and only one of me, but I will take some of you with me. Who wants to go first?" The crowd parted, and he got in his vehicle and drove away. They never bothered him again.

1955. He joined the army. In 1957, he was captured by the Vietnamese and put into a hole in the ground covered with bamboo sticks, where he was pissed on by his captors and fed slop handed to him on a pole let down through the gaps in the poles. One night, his captors got reckless and left the pole that they used to feed him with, in the pit. Jim shinnied up that pole and killed all three. He took their clothes as he was naked and ran into the jungle for three days and nights, surviving by camouflaging himself in the environment. When he finally saw humans, they thought he was the enemy because of said clothing, but he succeeded in waving to them and hollering American! He said, "It's a good thing they were a bad shot."

1955. After recuperating in Osaka, Japan, for two months, Jim decided to feel frisky and try riding a motorcycle in a barrel, which was wrecked. He survived, but it was very dangerous.

1956. While working on a helicopter H119 Squadron, air rescue Honeywell system, Jim was up on a scaffold fourteen feet off the ground working on the fuel injection mixture. The engine misfired right at the end of the exhaust, which ignited, and he fell eight feet, causing the damage he still has to this day: his hearing became problematic after hitting his head on the tire of the plane. The other guy working with him fell and hit his tailbone and died on the way to the hospital.

1970. Jim bought a farm in Union County, Tennessee. A neighbor's pig (evidentially "prize pig") came down and tore up the door to the house, so Jim killed the pig. The neighbor got angry and confronted him with a gun. Jim got out and threatened to draw on him (he had his own gun). The neighbor got frustrated and told Jim, "Go to hell. I'll take care of you." He got in his vehicle and drove off. Later, Jim would find out that same neighbor had hired a hit man (a guy named Murphy) for five hundred fifty dollars. He found out the man's name, went to his house, and told him, "Let's get this over with!"

The hired hit man said, "I'm giving him his damn money back! You go on and leave me the hell alone!"

So Jim asked, "Is that the end of it?"

He replied, "Any man crazy enough to confront me, I want nothin' to do with! That's the end of it."

1986. While helping his brother open a new barber shop Jim had to go out to the edge of the highway and remove a man hole cover in order to help turn the water on… He needed a tool that he didn't have and while going to get it; just after he got up…a car wrecked right over same man hole…

1991. In September, while working for the PST trucking company as terminal manager, Jim, wearing dress shoes (short on help and not expecting to have to do this particular job), was throwing skids off the back of a truck, slipped, and broke his neck. He didn't find out until January 1992 that his neck was broken and had been seeing a chiropractor who stopped adjusting his neck immediately! He was operated on in June and again in July because of a spinal fluid leak of thirty-six hours.

2017. After stopping at a store and then pulling out into traffic to go North, he waited for two cars to pass from behind. Just as he went to pull forward, he was hit head-on, from the left, by a 1974 full-sized GMC pickup truck, knocking him in his five-thousand-pound Ford Expedition forty feet into the air and ending up going the opposite way. He was knocked out, and the airbags did not deploy, but he came to and had the where-withal to put the vehicle in park as he coasted downhill, back-ward, into the Kroger parking lot. He sustained injuries to his spleen and three broken ribs on his right side, and they put a stent in his heart. Both vehicles were totaled. The driver of the other vehicle, an illegal alien, was not hurt; but the two women with him had to be transported in ambulances to the hospital.

2018. While standing near his mailbox and reading his just-retrieved mail, a seventeen-year-old student, who was trying to impress his girlfriend by driving too fast around a corner, hit the mailbox and slung it way up into the yard, missing Jim and causing him to fling himself out of the way or be killed. Jim got the license and reported to 911. A police officer, Michael Walter, came; and the young student returned with his mother in another vehicle and begged not to be put to jail for the felony of hit and run. Jim only wanted his mailbox fixed to his exact specifications. The police officer told the young man that "this man owns you." The young man fixed the mailbox, and Jim did not press charges. Police Officer Michael Walter said, "Jim could've ruined that boy's life, but Jim showed mercy and spared him, loss of license, years in prison, and not able to get insurance." The student's mother said, "He'll never pull another trick like that again."

* * * * *

I don't think anyone can say God was not in all of this, just as he is in all of our lives. I want this book to be an example to all that they too can overcome. Just listen to that still small voice and know that God is God, and he is in control, if one lets him. It's all about *choice*.

Who are we to say how God should work things? Daniel 4:25 states, "You will live like the wild animals. You will eat grass just as cattle do… Seven periods of time will pass by for you. Then you will recognize that the Most High God rules over all of the kingdoms of men. He gives them to anyone he wants" (https://bible.org/seriespage/9-god-humbles-nebuchadnezzar-Daniel-4). What had been said about me came true at once. I was driven away from people. I ate grass just as cattle do.

When I met Jim the first time, he was leaving a marriage that God did not intend for him to be in, but it led him to me and me to him as I was not in a marriage I should have been in. God moves in mysterious ways. Jim also drove a little red truck when I first met him. He has a bigger red truck this time. We started out living in a small trailer. This time we are living in a camper. And I have a car, so we're moving on up. LOL. God is giving us a second chance at what he intended, and this time, it will be as an example for others to *trust God*. When I first got back with Jim, in July, the magazine that I buy every week, *Woman's World*, had an article in it stating that Marie Osmond had remarried her first husband after twenty-five years! Not only that, in the game What Happened First, one of the choices was one of my favorite movies of all time, *The Parent Trap*, with Hayley Mills. Another one of my favorite movies is *It's a Wonderful Life*. These movies spoke to me. Were they signs for me to believe for a better future? Everyone has something that they cling to or spur them on and give them hope. There are things that speak to our own specific soul all the time.

There are signs everywhere for the believer.

Someone once asked me if I were a saint. I replied, "I just try to treat people the way I want to be treated, remembering my spiritual gifts and using them—exhortation, prophecy, mercy—and using my teaching here to help others. I'm believing for bigger things than me."

In this life, it's what we give away that we shall take with us to heaven. This life is but a vapor.

Hameroff's words suggest that human souls are much more than mere interactions of neurons in the brain. In fact, this theory indicates that these souls could have existed since the very beginning of time itself. And with all of the recent discoveries pertaining to dark energy and dark matter—substances that humans cannot see or interact with, but substances that we know exist, nevertheless—this theory could end up explaining things that are even more mysterious and fascinating.

This content was inspired by an amazing article that can be found here: https://www.peacequarters.com/scientists-found-soul-doesnt-die-goes-back-universe/.

"Whereas ye know not what shall be on the morrow. For what is your life? It is even as a vapor, that appeareth for a little time, and then vanisheth away" (James 4:14).

"Choose Wisely, Grasshopper." ("Kung Fu" was a TV series in the 1970's. As a pupil at a Monastery learning the art of Kung Fu, a very young David Carradine playing the lead character was known to his Master by a pet name and was told to 'Choose wisely, Grasshopper'.)

* * * * *

This is the picture of the angel Gabriel that Jim drew, as close to what he could depict, after Gabriel appeared to him in our bedroom along with our personal angels. We had three miracles about three weeks later.

ABOUT THE AUTHOR

Although the author is going on seventy years of age, her heart is perpetually young, which is renewed daily by her faith. She considers this book to be God's book that he has written through her life, which is still ongoing! LOL. She realizes that all of us are writing our own books. We all have a story to tell. Ever since she was a child of eight, she has wanted to be a part of the solution and not the problem. She believes that even the worst of the worst examples of people are loved by God and used as an example of what not to be. God tells us in his Word that he has a plan for all of us to be overcomers. When she looks back, she realizes that she has, indeed, overcome a lot of negatives and continues to pray for God's strength and wisdom as well as peace. She gives all the glory to God as he continues to use her, as a willing earthly vessel, for his plan.

9 781098 046040